Praise for
Courage in the Sheer Silence

"*Courage in the Sheer Silence* is a tour de force, an eye-opening journey into the powers that maintain racial inequality and injustice and the deep costs paid by those who choose to resist. This book reveals in stunning detail how the evil principality of racial injustice is no respecter of race. White leaders who speak against it will be silenced, shunned, pushed out, and defrocked. Wes Crawford gives voice to those forgotten for doing what was right, and in so doing, he gives us direction and courage to do what is right today."

—**Dr. Michael O. Emerson,** Chavanne Fellow in Religion and Public Policy, the Baker Institute for Public Policy at Rice University, and coauthor of *Divided by Faith* and *The Religion of Whiteness*

"Unacknowledged racism has a tendency to fester, and this remarkable book, *Courage in the Sheer Silence*, brings us face-to-face with racism, both overt and silent, within the Churches of Christ. With astute analysis building on prodigious research, Wes Crawford weaves the major events of the civil rights movement with the churches' response—or lack thereof. Consistent with the Christian theme of redemption, the author also introduces us to the 'small company of crusaders' who courageously confronted the issue."

—**Randall Balmer,** John Phillips Professor in Religion, Dartmouth College, and author of *Bad Faith: Race and the Rise of the Religious Right*

"Along with a heritage of support for the legalized subjugation of African Americans, the Churches of Christ consistently endorsed a racial status quo that perpetrated the lie of Black inferiority. Notwithstanding the presence of Black Christians within this majority White ecclesia, nothing resembling equality governed their status. Wes Crawford, a talented scholar of Church of Christ history and the author of compelling publications about African Americans and the Church of Christ, explores a cadre of dissenters who challenged their denomination to renounce their collusion in the sin of racism. Crawford's book is an objective but passionately written chapter in American religious history."

—**Dennis C. Dickerson,** PhD, Reverend James Lawson Chair of History, Emeritus, Vanderbilt University

"We need capable historians such as Dr. Wes Crawford to draw back the curtains of our past in Churches of Christ and reveal the events of the time in order to refine our present course. The theme of race relations in the church has too long been ignored. Wes shows not only how twentieth-century events shed light on that period of time, but also how they impact our present view of this important spiritual issue. Our American culture and past can be a profound retardant to our spiritual growth. A must-read!"
—**Dr. Royce Money,** President Emeritus, Abilene Christian University

"In *Courage in the Sheer Silence,* Wes Crawford delivers a profound exploration of truth that shatters Christians' historically quiet complicity in the face of racism. This book is not just timely; it is essential. With eye-opening research and a powerful, unwavering voice, Crawford provides a guiding light in the profound darkness of our times, *Courage in the Sheer Silence* is a must-read—a profoundly brave work that reminds us that silence can be broken, and healing, though long overdue, can still find a way."
—**Jerry Taylor,** Founder, Emancipation Fellowship Ministries; Associate Professor of Bible and Ministry, Abilene Christian University; Director, Carl Spain Center of Race Studies and Spiritual Action

Courage in the Sheer Silence

Courage in the Sheer Silence

Challenging
Racism in
20th-Century
Churches
of Christ

WES CRAWFORD

COURAGE IN THE SHEER SILENCE

Challenging Racism in 20th-Century Churches of Christ

Copyright © 2025 by Wes Crawford

ISBN 978-1-68426-013-3

Printed in the United States of America

Cataloging-in-Publication Data is on file at the Library of Congress, Washington, DC.

Cover design by Bruce Gore
Interior text design by Sandy Armstrong, Strong Design

For information, contact:
Abilene Christian University Press
ACU Box 29138
Abilene, Texas 79699

1-877-816-4455
www.acupressbooks.com

25 26 27 28 29 30 31 // 7 6 5 4 3 2 1

Contents

Introduction

The predominant response of Church of Christ leaders to the US civil rights movement of the 1950s and 1960s was silence. Most other Christian denominations found direction from formal pronouncements, such as the 1958 *Discrimination and Christian Conscience* document signed by Catholic bishops in the United States. In 1950, the General Assembly of the Presbyterian Church officially voted to end the practice of segregation within its synods.[1] Lacking any centralized denominational body to make such pronouncements on racism or segregation, Churches of Christ found informal and unofficial direction through their colleges, journals, and lectureships.[2] Well-known and respected Church of Christ preacher and college administrator William S. Banowsky once called the lectureship held annually on the

---

[1] Carolyn Dupont, "Reflections on Religion and the Civil Rights Movement," *OUPblog* (blog), April 4, 2016, https://blog.oup.com/2016/04/religion-civil-rights-movement/.

[2] Church of Christ lectureships, often, but not exclusively, held on the campuses of Church of Christ colleges, bring together well-known and respected preachers and teachers of the denomination who offer keynote addresses and classes to denominational members. During the 1950s and 1960s, these lectureships drew crowds into the thousands each year.

campus of Abilene Christian College the "mirror of a movement," insinuating that by examining the classes and sermons offered at that event, one could adequately understand the identity of the entire denomination.[3] Assuming the validity of Banowsky's thesis, one could reasonably conclude Churches of Christ paid scant attention to the civil rights movement. Indeed, if one's only window into American culture in the 1950s and 1960s were lectureships associated with Churches of Christ, one would never know about the civil rights revolution that ignited the country. Church of Christ lectureships, journals, and colleges remained virtually silent, and some members of the denomination surely viewed that silence as a virtue.

History lavishes praise on silence. The Greek philosopher Plutarch once declared, "A sage thing is timely silence, and better than any speech."[4] Perhaps the best-known and most influential English playwright, William Shakespeare, said, "The silence, often of pure innocence, persuades where speaking fails."[5] Legend suggests that the ancient Chinese philosopher Confucius praised silence as "a true friend that never betrays." Henry Wadsworth Longfellow, the famed American poet, called silence "the great peacemaker."[6]

Silence, as they say, is golden. Nevertheless, moments do arise when silence causes harm. During the opening decades of the twenty-first century, stories surfaced about sexual abuse within the Catholic church. A grand jury in Pennsylvania accused hundreds of priests of abusing

---

[3] William S. Banowsky, *The Mirror of a Movement: Churches of Christ as Seen through the Abilene Christian College Lectureship* (Christian Publishing, 1965). On the use of "denomination" in this book, I am using the word based on Sidney Mead's definition: "a voluntary association of like-hearted and like-minded individuals, who are united on the basis of common beliefs for the purpose of accomplishing tangible and defined objectives." Sidney E. Mead, *The Lively Experiment: The Shaping of Christianity in America* (Harper & Row, 1963), 104.

[4] "The Education of Children," in *Plutarch: Moralia*, vol. 1, trans. Frank Cole Babbitt (Harvard University Press, 1927), 51.

[5] William Shakespeare, *The Winter's Tale*, ed. Barbara A. Mowat and Paul Werstine (Simon & Schuster, 2005), Act 2, Scene 2.

[6] Henry Wadsworth Longfellow, *The Works of Henry Wadsworth Longfellow* (Wordsworth Editions, 1998), 410.

"more than a thousand children over seven decades."[7] As the abuse continued, church bishops remained silent, and some even took steps to conceal the crimes. In her book, *The Crime and the Silence*, Anna Bikont reports the shocking events that took place in Jedwabne, a small town in Poland, on July 10, 1941. On that date, citizens of this small town rounded up their Jewish population and burned them alive in a barn. Almost as astonishing as the crime itself, the surviving residents of Jedwabne kept silent about the murders for more than sixty years. Bikont's book underscores the powerful and damaging effects of silence on individuals and a society.

One of the most curious statements concerning silence comes from the pages of the Bible. First Kings 18–19 records the mountainous height and the deepest valley of Elijah's prophetic career. In a moment of triumph, Elijah, the prophet of God, met 450 prophets of Baal on Mount Carmel for a showdown of epic proportions. Elijah and the prophets of Baal each built an altar of wood and placed portions of a bull on it, but they refrained from adding fire. All contestants petitioned their gods to send fire upon the altar. Baal's prophets cried out to their god first, shouting and even cutting themselves in an effort to draw his attention. After several hours, "there was no voice, no answer, and no response" (1 Kings 18:29). Following their failed attempt, Elijah seized the opportunity to grab a decisive victory for Yahweh. Elijah prayed, and Yahweh immediately sent fire from heaven so powerful that it consumed the meat and even incinerated the stones surrounding the altar. Yahweh and Yahweh's prophet Elijah stood tall as the unambiguous victors in the holy contest on Mount Carmel.

Immediately after the victory, Elijah led the people to slaughter the 450 prophets of Baal in the Kishon Valley, and this action drew the eye of Jezebel, a Baal worshiper and queen of Israel. She made a vow to take Elijah's life within one day, and Elijah ran away. The champion of

---

[7] Mary Schmich, "When Priests Abuse, We Shouldn't Keep Silent. Tell Your Story," *Chicago Tribune*, August 21, 2018, https://www.chicagotribune.com/2018/08/21/when-priests-abuse-we-shouldnt-keep-silent-tell-your-story/.

Mount Carmel fled to Horeb, the same mountain upon which Moses had received the Ten Commandments. Yahweh found Elijah at Horeb and asked him, "What are you doing here, Elijah?" (1 Kings 19:13). The prophet offered a pitiful reply, lamenting his perception that he alone remained among the persecuted prophets of Yahweh. Following Elijah's lament, Yahweh spoke:

> "Go out and stand on the mountain before the Lord, for the Lord is about to pass by." Now there was a great wind, so strong that it was splitting mountains and breaking rocks in pieces before the Lord, but the Lord was not in the wind, and after the wind an earthquake, but the Lord was not in the earthquake, and after the earthquake a fire, but the Lord was not in the fire, and after the fire a sound of sheer silence. When Elijah heard it, he wrapped his face in his mantle and went out and stood at the entrance of the cave. (1 Kings 19:11–13)

The wind, earthquake, and fire served only as the procession traveling ahead of Yahweh's presence. Elijah knew to cover his head and to exit the cave to meet Yahweh only when the sheer silence arrived. Although humans are tempted to search for God amidst the loud and boisterous and terrifying, God sometimes meets humanity in moments of silence.

Loud and boisterous (and sometimes terrifying) figures dominated the American religious landscape in the middle decades of the twentieth century, and many of those clamorous characters provided leadership to Churches of Christ. Larger-than-life personalities, such as Foy Wallace Jr., and powerful editors, such as Reuel Lemmons and Benton Cordell Goodpasture, used their seats of influence to trumpet their positions on God, Scripture, and culture. Their silence on matters related to race and racism may lead students of the denomination to assume Churches of Christ had nothing to say about the civil rights movement; nevertheless, this volume encourages those students to listen more carefully. Although the major publications, institutions, and leaders did not lend their voices to the racial revolution, a few courageous preachers did speak out of this silence, and their voices provided a prophetic word of the Lord to their contemporaries and to subsequent generations willing to listen.

At the outset of this volume, three questions need clear answers. First, *Why does this book ignore women?* Certainly, women also provided their voices to the questions surrounding race and racism throughout the twentieth century. Undoubtedly, some of those voices spoke words with courage, not unlike Carl Spain, John Allen Chalk, Walter Burch, Dwain Evans, and Bud Stumbaugh, and most women (like their male counterparts) remained completely silent. This book does not address the voices of women for two important reasons. First, the sources simply do not exist. Throughout the twentieth century, Churches of Christ disallowed women places of congregational or denominational leadership; therefore, as one scans the historical record searching for the voices of women from lectureship speeches, journal articles, or sermons preached at local congregations, one comes up empty.

Ona Belknap, editor of *Christian Woman*, noticed this issue in June 1968, and she sought to correct that injustice even then. Not long after the race relations workshop that took place in Atlanta during the summer of 1968 (an event that will receive considerable attention in this book), she wrote a letter to Chalk about her inability to contribute her wisdom to that gathering of men. She wrote in that letter, simply, "I was told I could not attend the meeting in Atlanta last week because I am a woman."[8] She went on to express her frustration throughout the letter, and she finally added:

> It may not be ladylike or discreet to raise these questions
> right on top of the racial questions that are rife now—but they
> are almost one and the same—at least they both share segre-
> gation and the feeling they are discriminated against. We are
> tired of hemming diapers for the African babies who do not

---

[8] Ona Belknap to John Allen Chalk, 28 June 1968, John Allen Chalk: Personal Correspondence, Harding School of Theology, https://scholarworks.harding.edu/cgi/viewcontent.cgi?article=7264&context=hst-chalk-personal.

> wear diapers. We are tired of using our intellect in keeping
> the size 36 from the size 40 baptismal garments.[9]

Generations from now, when historians write about twenty-first-century Churches of Christ, they will have at their disposal numerous documents, sermons, and monographs written and presented by women, but until then, contemporary historians must rely on the artifacts left behind by men.

The second reason this book does not lend an ear to the voices of women is related to the first. This volume seeks to address the power structures of the denomination, and Church of Christ women did not occupy positions of power in the twentieth century. The most visible seats of power within Churches of Christ (journals, lectureships, colleges, and prominent congregations) found leadership solely from men. This book argues that the most prominent leaders of the denomination (all of them men) remained silent on issues related to race and racism and worked to suppress the voices of those who attempted to break that silence.

This book focuses on the most influential power structures of the denomination that shaped Church of Christ orthodoxy, but one hopes to see additional studies in the future that will unearth the work of local congregational members who suppressed prophetic voices, remained silent on these issues, or vocalized their dissatisfaction with the racist status quo. Loretta Hunnicutt, professor of history at Pepperdine University, continues her difficult and important study on women within the Stone–Campbell Movement, and her work, as well as the work of others, will begin to make audible the important voices of women.

The second question that demands an answer is, *Why does this book only tell the stories of White men?* Although most White leaders within Churches of Christ remained silent during the tumultuous days of the civil rights movement, numerous courageous Black leaders screamed

---

[9] Belknap to Chalk, 28 June 1968.

into that silence. Richard Nathaniel Hogan, longtime influential editor of *The Christian Echo*, lambasted White college administrators for refusing to integrate their campuses years following *Brown v. Board of Education*.[10] Fred Gray, graduate of Nashville Christian Institute, student of Marshall Keeble, and famed civil rights attorney for both Rosa Parks and Martin Luther King Jr., stood front and center during the civil rights movement. In his book *Strive toward Freedom*, in which he told the story of the Montgomery bus boycott, King described Gray as "the brilliant young Negro who later became the chief counsel for the protest movement."[11] Jack Evans, another graduate of Nashville Christian Institute and president of Southwestern Christian College (the only predominantly Black college associated with Churches of Christ) for nearly fifty years, regularly spoke and wrote about the problem of racism within the denomination, and he helped raise more than a generation of Black preachers who continued that strategy.[12] Floyd Rose, a classmate of both Gray and Evans at Nashville Christian Institute, eventually moved to Toledo, Ohio, and spent his adult life as a civil rights activist. He served as president of the National Association for the Advancement of Colored People (NAACP) in Toledo and took on some of the largest corporations in the United States for their discriminatory practices (including Macy's and Coca-Cola).[13]

Edward J. Robinson has spent the last decade-plus producing excellent books describing the heroic careers of numerous Black leaders within Churches of Christ, but scant attention has been given to the ways in which White denominational leaders addressed (or failed to

---

[10] See, for example, R. N. Hogan, "Brother David Lipscomb Stood with God on Race Prejudice in the Church of Christ," *Christian Echo* 55 (June 1960): 2–3; "Is It Law or Down-Right Prejudice?" *Christian Echo* 58 (June 1963): 3; "Tradition Versus Commandments," *Christian Echo* 58 (July 1963): 1, 5.

[11] James A. Washington, ed., *A Testament of Hope: The Essential Writings and Speeches of Martin Luther King Jr.* (Harper San Francisco, 1986), 431.

[12] See Edward J. Robinson, *Hard-Fighting Soldiers: A History of African American Churches of Christ* (University of Tennessee Press, 2019), 151–55.

[13] Wes Crawford, "An Apple That Fell Far from Its Tree: The Protest Legacy of Floyd Rose," *Restoration Quarterly* 63, no. 1 (First Quarter 2021): 11–18.

address) the racism existent within their movement.[14] This volume adds to the excellent scholarship of Robinson by turning attention to White leaders within Churches of Christ. The present volume provides a more complete picture of Churches of Christ by bringing into focus the ways in which the most prominent leaders of the denomination engaged (or failed to engage) the effects of racism in their ranks.

The third and final question demanding an answer is: *Why does this book only tell the stories of White preachers and editors?* This book does not deeply examine the important activism of Don Haymes, an activist and scholar within Churches of Christ who routinely criticized denominational leaders for failing to address the most pressing issues of the 1960s while instead focusing on restoring first-century church practices. He suggested the denomination had "managed to sidetrack the real issues in a desperate search for gnats to strain."[15] These pages do not tell the detailed story of Everett Ferguson, a White student at Abilene Christian College (who later become a world-renowned early church historian), who encouraged the school to desegregate during a chapel address delivered in 1953 (the year before the Supreme Court mandate).[16] Another person this book does not tell about in depth is Robert Randolph, who served as a dean at Massachusetts Institute of Technology for many decades and ended his career there as the campus chaplain from 2007 until he retired in 2016. Before his career, Randolph attended Abilene Christian College, and throughout his adult life, he provided leadership to the Brookline Church of Christ, a congregation near Boston, Massachusetts, that consistently challenged gender and racial inequality, often at the urging of Randolph. In addition to these

---

[14] See Edward J. Robinson, *To Save My Race from Abuse: The Life of Samuel Robert Cassius* (University of Alabama Press, 2007); *Show Us How You Do It: Marshall Keeble and the Rise of Black Churches of Christ in the United States, 1914–1968* (University of Alabama Press, 2008); *The Fight Is On in Texas: A History of African American Churches of Christ in the Lone Star State, 1865–2000* (Abilene Christian University Press, 2008); *I Was Under a Burden: The Life of Annie C. Tuggle* (Abilene Christian University Press, 2011); *Hard-Fighting Soldiers*.

[15] Don Haymes, "The Church of the Gospels," *Mission* 2, no. 6 (Dec. 1968): 10.

[16] Barclay Key, *Race and Restoration: Churches of Christ and the Black Freedom Struggle* (Louisiana State University Press, 2020), 77.

few, hundreds and perhaps thousands of other names could be listed among the champions for civil rights within congregations associated with Churches of Christ. This book, however, focuses on influential preachers, educators, and editors who occupied roles that enabled them to steer the denomination in certain directions—either toward or away from racial equality.

In addition to these three important questions, this introduction addresses a key term used throughout this book—*denomination*. Those familiar with the history of Churches of Christ appreciate the complex relationship Churches of Christ have shared with this label. In the nineteenth century, Alexander Campbell, Barton W. Stone, and others set out to eradicate the divisions within the church by calling all Christians to leave their denominations and merge instead into the one true church. Since that time, many leaders and members of Churches of Christ have resisted applying this label to their religious movement, opting instead to refer to their group as simply the church, movement, or tradition. In employing the term *denomination* throughout this volume, this book does not mean to make an important theological claim. Rather, *denomination* is the most accurate and appropriate term to describe any movement, fellowship, or tradition within the larger church.

In 1963, church historian Sidney Mead defined a denomination as "a voluntary association of like-hearted and like-minded individuals, who are united on the basis of common beliefs for the purpose of accomplishing tangible and defined objectives."[17] Churches of Christ (much like Baptists, Methodists, and Presbyterians) fit this description well. One should also acknowledge the irony inherent in this issue. Historically, most members of Churches of Christ resisted the label of "denomination" because they believed they alone had restored the one true church. Although members of Christian denominations had purportedly failed in their efforts to live up to the vision of the church cast from the pages of the New Testament, leaders and members of Churches of Christ had supposedly succeeded. This volume will show

---

[17] Mead, *Lively Experiment*, 104.

that at least on the issue of race, White members of Churches of Christ behaved much like their national counterparts within the Methodist, Baptist, and Presbyterian denominations.

The book exists in two parts. Part One attempts to provide some context for twentieth-century Churches of Christ. This section examines three groups of people: those who openly expressed their belief in White supremacy (especially Foy Wallace Jr.), those who remained deaf to the sounds of racism within Churches of Christ (especially Reuel Lemmons and Benton Cordell Goodpasture), and those who knew racism existed but remained silent (especially James Fowler). These groups of people helped create the racist culture of twentieth-century Churches of Christ. Not only did they create this environment with their speech, but they also deliberately and strategically silenced other voices who sought to steer the denomination away from its racist roots.

Part Two tells the stories of several White leaders who spoke out against the racist status quo of Churches of Christ and paid the price for their courage. Following their activism, these leaders lost their jobs, had speaking invitations cancelled, and endured threats against their lives, and most of them exited ministry altogether and chose to take less dangerous vocational paths. Because most of their ministerial careers lasted only a short time and because White denominational leaders and institutions worked to silence their voices, their stories remain largely unknown. This volume seeks to right a wrong by resurrecting their monumental acts of courage. Carl Spain, Walter Burch, John Allen Chalk, Dwain Evans, and Bud Stumbaugh challenged the church they loved to become more like Jesus. In telling their stories, this book seeks to help its readers do the same.

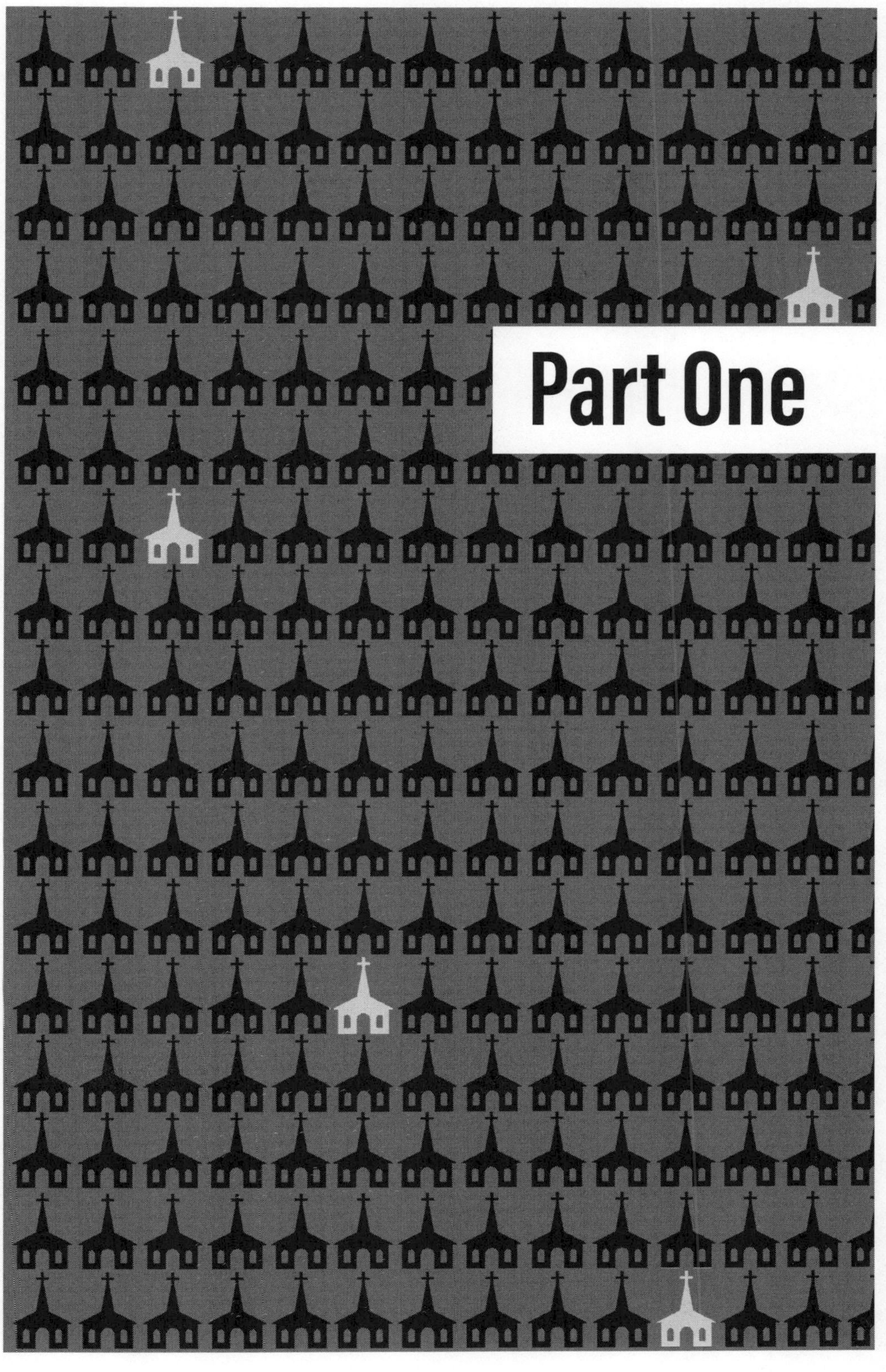

Part One

The Voice of Supremacy

Although most White leaders within Churches of Christ remained silent during the turbulent days of the US civil rights movement, the sounds of racism trumpeted loudly across the history of the denomination. Alexander Campbell, one of the founders of the Stone–Campbell Movement, wrote in 1845:

> For myself, I greatly prefer the condition and the prospects of the Free to the Slave States; especially as respects the white portion of their population. Much as I may sympathize with a black man, I love the white man more. As a political economist, and as a philanthropist, I have many reasons for preferring the prospects and condition of the Free to the Slave Sates; but especially, as a Christian, I sympathize much more with the owners of slaves, their heirs, and successors, than with the slaves which they possess and bequeathe [*sic*].

Campbell plainly revealed his White supremacist ideology and tied this point of view to his Christian identity. As a Christian, Campbell wrote, he sympathized more with slaveholders (Whites) than with slaves (Blacks). Such statements by the founder of the Movement provided seeds for the racism that would continue to grow within the denomination for more than two centuries. Not surprisingly, as multiple Stone–Campbell Movement historians have reported, by the dawn of the US Civil War, those involved with the Stone–Campbell Movement held 101,000 slaves, making it (per capita) the largest slave-owning religious body in the United States. Only Methodists and Baptists held more slaves overall than members of Campbell's Movement.[1]

The seeds of racism planted by Campbell in the mid-nineteenth century germinated and sprouted at various moments throughout history, including the 1922 fall gospel meeting in Abilene, Texas. On the last night of the lectureship that took place on the campus of Abilene Christian College, as then president Jesse P. Sewell presided at the pulpit in front of the auditorium, ten members of the Ku Klux Klan in full regalia paraded down the middle aisle and handed Sewell an envelope and a message to read to the assembled crowd. Sewell took the envelope and read the message aloud to the congregation. Through their note, the Klansmen thanked Abilene Christian College for hosting the meeting, which they viewed as a "great benefit to our community," and urged them to accept their donation of twenty-five dollars. Not only did Sewell oblige the Knights of the Ku Klux Klan by reading their message; he also accepted their donation.[2] Upon receiving criticism

---

[1] See Winfred E. Garrison and Alfred T. DeGroot, *The Disciples of Christ* (Christian Board of Publications, 1948), 468; David Edwin Harrell, *Quest for a Christian America, 1800–65: A Social History of the Disciples of Christ*, vol. 1 (University of Alabama Press, 2003), 93, first published in 1966 by Disciples of Christ Historical Society; D. Newell Williams, Douglas A. Foster, and Paul M. Blowers, eds., *The Stone–Campbell Movement: A Global History* (Chalice Press, 2013), 38. The above historians draw their conclusions from the *Annual Report of the American and Foreign* Anti-Slavery *Society* (William Harned, Office Agent, 1851), 56.

[2] One should note that a similar event occurred in the mid-1920s when Foy E. Wallace Jr. preached at a meeting in Oklahoma City. On that occasion, Wallace refused to accept the money and demanded that the members of the Ku Klux Klan take the "pillowcases from their heads" and identify themselves. This event is not discussed in this chapter because it appears to have less to say about Wallace's racial ideology than his desire for his audience's attention. The Knights of the Ku Klux Klan interrupted his meeting, and he chastised them for it. For a fuller description of this event, see J. T. Marlin, "Foy E. Wallace, Jr.: The Prince of Preachers Passes On! Ku Klux Klan Rebuffed in Oklahoma City," *The Christian Journal* 37, no. 2 (Feb. 1980): 10.

for his actions by certain Abilene Christian College board of trustees members, Sewell unconvincingly asserted that he did not know anything about the Ku Klux Klan, so he had refrained from making any public judgments about them during the 1922 gathering.[3] Jefferson Davis Tant, one of the foremost leaders among early twentieth-century Church of Christ preachers, praised Sewell for his attitude toward the Ku Klux Klan and encouraged other church members to support their work as well.[4]

The racist behavior of Church of Christ members mirrored the behavior of Christians from other Southern denominations. Some historians of American religion suggest the sectarian and nonpolitical posture of Churches of Christ distanced them from membership in national political organizations, such as the Ku Klux Klan.[5] Yet, Jason Fikes rightly counters that the radical autonomy of the denomination contributed to tremendous diversity among its membership.[6] Lacking an authoritative or official governing body to guide them away from or toward any organization, members of Churches of Christ behaved much like Southern Baptists or Methodists. Regardless of their membership in any organization, evidence suggests Church of Christ leaders and laypersons exhibited racist behavior, much like their regional counterparts.

Unfortunately, a careful study of Church of Christ history uncovers numerous heinous examples of overt, public racism. Nicholas Brodie Hardeman cofounded (along with Arvy G. Freed) the institution that came to be known as Freed-Hardeman University. The highlight of Hardeman's illustrious preaching career came between 1922 and 1942, when he preached a series of sermons in the historic Ryman Auditorium in Nashville, Tennessee. The Ryman, which served as the home for the

---

[3] See Jason Fikes, "Jesse P. Sewell, White Supremacy, and the Formative Years of Abilene Christian College," *Restoration Quarterly* 64, no. 3 (Third Quarter 2022): 170–81.

[4] Fikes, "Jesse P. Sewell," 176; Jefferson Davis Tant, "Are We Doing Wrong?" *Firm Foundation* 40, no. 40 (Jan. 2, 1923): 3.

[5] Walter Buenger, *The Path to a Modern South: Northeast Texas between Reconstruction and the Great Depression* (University of Texas Press, 2001), 207; Linda Gordon, *The Second Coming of the KKK: The Ku Klux Klan of the 1920s and the American Political Tradition* (Liveright, 2017), 88.

[6] Fikes, "Jesse P. Sewell," 175–76.

Grand Ole Opry from 1943 until 1974, originally housed the Union Gospel Tabernacle, and for many years thereafter, it hosted religious gatherings and entertainment events. The Southern Baptist Convention convened at the Ryman, Booker T. Washington once delivered a lecture from its stage, and the Fisk Jubilee Singers graced the stage back in 1892. On five separate occasions (1922, 1923, 1928, 1938, and 1942), Hardeman delivered a series of sermons to between six and eight thousand people each night, with as many as two or three thousand turned away. The lectures solidified his place on the "Mount Rushmore of preachers" within Churches of Christ. Like many other White preachers from his era, Hardeman exhibited racist behavior. He refused to shake hands with Black attendees at his meetings.[7] After placing his entire racist legacy under a microscope, in 2019, Oklahoma Christian University presented the Hardeman Auditorium with a new name, the Baugh Auditorium (named after Benton and Paula Baugh). The name change occurred because the university administration recognized the racist ideology of Hardeman and hoped to erase that name from one of the most prominent buildings on their campus.[8]

Another well-known educator of the denomination, George Stuart Benson, also displayed racism throughout his long career. Benson became a household name among members of Churches of Christ when he served as President of Harding College from 1936 until 1965, but he also spent many years as a missionary to China and became a prominent champion for capitalism and democracy in the early years of the Cold War between the United States and the Soviet Union.[9] Years following the 1954 decision of the Supreme Court to desegregate schools, Benson resisted this change at Harding College. During a 1957 address to the student body during chapel, revealing his belief in the

---

[7] Foy E. Wallace Jr., "Negro Meetings for White People," *Bible Banner* 3, no. 8 (1941): 7.

[8] Bobby Ross Jr., "Racial Concerns Prompt Renaming of Christian University's Auditorium," *BobbyRossJr* (blog), February 27, 2019, https://bobbyrossjr.com/2019/02/27/racial-concerns-prompt-renaming-of -oklahoma-christian-universitys-hardeman-auditorium/.

[9] See John C. Stevens, *Before Any Were Willing: The Story of George S. Benson* (Harding University, 1991), 152–64.

innate sexual savagery of Black persons, Benson suggested that integration would "increase destruction to properties, increase gonorrhea and syphilis, and increase pregnancies." In that same address, he said, "The blackbirds and bluebirds, the blue jays and mockingbirds, they don't mix and mingle together, young people!"[10] In 1963, at the height of the civil rights movement, Benson awarded an honorary doctorate to Senator John McClellan because of the politician's decision to oppose the desegregation of Central High School in Little Rock.[11] Not long after the death of George Floyd in 2020, Oklahoma Christian University made the decision to remove Benson's name from its administration building.[12]

Athens Clay Pullias, yet another prominent educator within Churches of Christ, served for many years as president of David Lipscomb College. Not unlike Benson, Pullias courted Southern politicians and expressed his pro-segregation feelings openly. He complained about having to shake hands with Marshall Keeble, the best-known Black evangelist among Churches of Christ.[13] Floyd Rose, another Black preacher within the denomination, sought admission to David Lipscomb College in 1963, but Pullias called the police and had him escorted off the campus. Interestingly, as Rose exited the campus while flanked by White police officers, a large contingent of White college students gathered and booed the officers.[14]

Regrettably, tales of racism abound from the annals of Churches of Christ. This chapter, however, centers primarily on the racist behavior of only one individual, who happened to be among the most influential preachers of twentieth-century Churches of Christ—namely, Foy Esco Wallace Jr.

---

[10] Zach Dailey, "A Year of Amazing Grace: Will Harding Look Back or Forge a New Path Forward?" *Odyssey*, September 12, 2016, http://www.theodysseyonline.com/year-of-amazing-grace/.

[11] Barclay Key, *Race and Restoration: Churches of Christ and the Black Freedom* Struggle (Louisiana State University Press, 2020), 94–95.

[12] Elise Miller, "George Benson's Name Removed from Administration Building," *Talon.News*, August 14, 2020, http://www.talon.news/news/geroge-bensons-name-removed-from-administration-building/.

[13] Key, *Race and Restoration*, 95.

[14] Key, *Race and Restoration*, 122.

American church historian Richard T. Hughes wrote of Wallace, "In the 1930s and 1940s, he emerged as the single most influential preacher in Churches of Christ."[15] Melvin Wise, a longtime preacher and writer in the denomination, referred to Wallace as "the Alexander Campbell of our age."[16] Ira Y. Rice Jr., another prominent Church of Christ preacher and an individual with whom Wallace sparred on numerous occasions within denominational periodicals, labeled Wallace the "Preacher Laureate of the twentieth century."[17] Noble Patterson and Terry J. Gardner coauthored a book about Wallace in 1999, and in addition to their own interpretations of Wallace's life, their volume includes numerous primary documents written by and about the "soldier of the cross" (the subtitle of their book and the moniker of Wallace etched on his gravestone). The opening pages of the book contain tributes written about Wallace by several well-known preachers, writers, and college administrators within Churches of Christ, including Willard Collins, J. T. Marlin, and Robert Taylor Jr. These testimonials attribute to Wallace such illustrious titles as "dean of gospel preachers," "guardian of the gospel," and "giant."[18]

Among twentieth-century leaders within Churches of Christ, Wallace had few equals. He served as editor or staff editor of the *Gospel Advocate* (1930–34), *The Gospel Guardian* (1935–36), *Firm Foundation* (1936–37), *Bible Banner* (1938–49), and *Torch* (1950–51). He also edited twelve books and participated in thirteen public religious debates. Wallace received most of his notoriety, however, from his ability in the pulpit. The son of a preacher, Foy E. Wallace Sr., young Wallace began his career as a pulpiteer in 1912 at age fifteen, and for the next half-century, he challenged, comforted, cajoled, and infuriated his audiences.

---

[15] Richard T. Hughes, *Reviving the Ancient Faith: The Story of Churches of Christ in America* (Eerdmans, 1996), 160–61.

[16] Melvin Wise, *The Christian Journal* 21, no. 2 (1980): front cover.

[17] Ira Y. Rice, "Foy E. Wallace, Jr., Preacher Laureate of the 20th Century, Breaks Silver Cord," *Contending for the Faith* 11, no. 2 (1980): 1.

[18] Noble Patterson and Terry Gardner, *Foy E. Wallace, Jr.: Soldier of the Cross* (Wallace Memorial Fund, 1999), iii–xi.

Although loved by many, Wallace had an equal number of adversaries. As Patterson and Gardner point out, "Wallace was involved in every major controversy in the churches of Christ from 1930 until his death at the close of 1979."[19] Those who have studied the twentieth-century history of this denomination may attest to its legion of theological controversies centering on issues ranging from premillennialism to nationalism to institutionalism. Wallace stood center stage as each of these debates raged loudly from the pulpits, journals, and colleges associated with Churches of Christ. In a well-crafted description of this preaching giant, Patterson and Gardner wrote, "Foy E. Wallace, Jr., was the most loved of preachers and the most hated. He was called the kindest of men and the most bitter. He was praised for his patience and condemned for his impatience in the superlative degree . . . Everyone who knew Wallace either loved him, hated him or loved and hated him at the same time."[20] Wallace's penchant for finding controversy placed him at the center of many theological debates throughout his lifetime. The topics of race, racism, and segregation did not thunder from the mouths of Church of Christ preachers nearly as often as the topics of premillennialism or institutionalism. Indeed, most pulpits remained silent on these subjects. Even Wallace spoke and wrote little on these topics, but the words he did offer allow historians to align his ideology with other Southern White racists of his era.

Writing in 1935, Wallace penned an article in *The Gospel Guardian* about evangelism. The article, "Convert Your Cook," encouraged his White readers to focus their evangelistic energies on converting those closest in proximity to them—namely, Black servants. Here is the entire text of his short piece:

> To reach the colored race, we do not have to go anywhere.
> They are here. We do not have to learn their language. They
> have already learned ours. We do not have to study their

---

[19] Patterson and Gardner, *Foy E. Wallace, Jr.*, 1.
[20] Patterson and Gardner, *Foy E. Wallace, Jr.*, 1.

> ways or manner of thought. We know them, and they have
> largely copied our own ways. There are more of them, and
> they are closer to us, and we have already made more
> headway, and have the means and equipment to preach the
> gospel to them with greater effect than to any group or race
> on earth, outside of our own white Americans, many of whom
> are still prospects. If one cannot work up a zeal for saving his
> own cook, or washwoman, or yardman, how can he claim to
> be "missionary minded," at all?[21]

With these brief comments, Wallace aligned himself with the White supremacist ideology prevalent during his lifetime (and throughout US history). He believed the English language belonged to White people and that Black people "learned" it over time. Keep in mind that Black Africans had come with White Europeans to America in the early seventeenth century, and by the time of Wallace's article, Black people in America had been speaking English for nearly 450 years! He assumed Black people made it a goal to copy the ways of White people. Finally, he lumped all Black people into a servant caste, labeling them cooks, washwomen, and yardmen. Wallace did not seek to prove these bold assumptions; rather, he assumed their validity and offered them without comment.

The racism so common in Wallace's speech found its genesis in a time long before he ascended any Church of Christ pulpit. The racial hierarchy evidenced in his words may have found its roots in Aristotle, but certainly by the eighteenth century, this ideology dominated the Euro–American mindset. By this era in history, as scientists set out to classify animals, planets, and diseases, they also began to classify human beings. Although they could have differentiated humans by numerous physical characteristics, these scientists latched onto the diversity brought about through skin color. They, separating human beings into different orders based on the pigment of their skin, also

---

[21] Foy Wallace, "Convert Your Cook," *The Gospel Guardian* 1, no. 1 (1935): 34.

began to rank those orders from highest to lowest. The highest order of human beings supposedly possessed greater intellectual ability than those of lower orders. Indeed, those beings making up the lowest strata of this so-called great chain of being were regarded as cursed and sexual savages who, left to their own agency, would regress to their natural bestial state. Not surprisingly, these Euro–American scientists placed Black people at the bottom of this great chain and placed themselves at the top.[22] For example, philosophers such as Voltaire argued that Black people represented a lower order of human beings than their White counterparts. Black-skinned people, in their natural state, he suggested, possessed a savage character and less innate intellectual ability.[23]

Scientists were not alone in perpetuating a racial hierarchy; theologians, biblical scholars, and church leaders also sought to justify their racism by appealing to the words of the Bible. Among the most effective tools used by Christians to support slavery in the United States during the antebellum period was a racist interpretation of Genesis 9:18–25, commonly referred to as "the curse of Ham." Christians have employed this interpretation to justify numerous atrocities, including the Crusades, the transatlantic slave trade, the Rwandan genocide, and American slavery and segregation.[24] As defined by David M. Goldenberg, the curse of Ham refers to "the belief that based on the story of Noah's cursing in Genesis 9, blacks have been afflicted with eternal servitude; in other words, the divinely sanctioned combination of black skin and slavery."[25] Although this theory has roots that could run as deep as the third century, the curse of Ham found renewed life in the days preceding the

---

[22] Winthrop Jordan, *White over Black: American Attitudes toward the Negro: 1550–1812* (W. W. Norton, 1968), 219–28, 482–511; Nathaniel Southgate Shaler, "The Negro Problem," *Atlantic Monthly* 54 (Nov. 1884): 703; Shaler, "Science and the African Problem," *Atlantic Monthly* 66 (July 1890): 42.

[23] See Scott F. Gilbert, "Systemic Racism, Systemic Sexism, and the Embryological Enterprise," *Developmental Biology* 473 (May 2021): 97–104; Jordan, *White over Black*, 219–28, 482–511; Wes Crawford, *Shattering the Illusion: How African American Churches of Christ Moved from Segregation to Independence* (Abilene Christian University Press, 2013), 10–17.

[24] For a list of sources detailing the ways in which the curse of Ham has been used to justify these atrocities, see Wongi Park, "The Blessing of Whiteness in the Curse of Ham: Reading Gen 9:18–29 in the Antebellum South," *Religions* 12, no. 11 (2021): 928.

[25] David M. Goldenberg, *Black and Slave: The Origins and History of the Curse of Ham* (De Gruyter, 2017), 5.

Civil War, as proponents of slavery sought divine justification for their political and cultural positions.

This racist ideology created and sustained by scientists and theologians dominated the Western world beginning in the eighteenth century. George M. Frederickson writes that racism "either directly sustains or proposes to establish a racial order, a permanent group hierarchy that is believed to reflect the laws of nature or the decrees of God."[26] When such racism becomes normative for an entire culture, such as the culture in which Wallace existed in the mid-twentieth century, institutional racism, or systemic racism (a term that first appeared in Stokely Carmichael [name changed to Kwame Ture in 1969] and Charles Hamilton's *Black Power: The Politics of Liberation* in 1967), results.

Other than his racist-ladened evangelistic advice, Wallace addressed the topic of race only once more in his published writings. This one article, however, speaks volumes about his views of Black people. Wallace published the article, "Negro Meetings for White People," in March 1941 in his periodical, the *Bible Banner*. (The entire article may be found in Appendix A in the back of this book.)

Numerous aspects of Wallace's character come to the foreground in this article, and chief among them was his jealousy of other preachers. In this brief column, Wallace displayed his jealousy of Richard Nathaniel Hogan (a well-known Black preacher and editor within Churches of Christ), Marshall Keeble (the most successful and respected twentieth-century Black evangelist of the denomination), and Ira Y. Rice (editor of the *Christian Soldier*). As this chapter shows, few twentieth-century Church of Christ preachers challenged him in notoriety and preaching acclaim, and the tributes written in his honor following his death provide evidence of the esteem in which many held him. Wallace's biography, written by Patterson and Gardner, records many of these tributes,[27] and certain periodicals, including

---

[26] George Frederickson, *Racism: A Short History* (Princeton University Press, 2002), 6.

[27] Patterson and Gardner, *Foy E. Wallace, Jr.*, iii–xi.

The Christian Journal, devoted entire commemorative issues to his memory following his death in 1979.[28] In spite of his reputation, however, Wallace modeled remarkable jealousy of his preaching peers. This article describes a man seething with jealousy as Rice, Hogan, and Keeble grew in their effectiveness and influence as preachers within Churches of Christ. Wallace could barely entertain the possibility that the young editor of the *Christian Soldier* garnered attention for his preaching meeting, and he rejected outright the possibility that "any negro" could measure up to him in the pulpit.[29]

Hiding just beneath his jealousy and criticism of Hogan and Keeble were notions of racial superiority. The last line of his article clearly records his position on this matter: "And if any of the white brethren get worked up over what I have said, and want to accuse me of being jealous of the negro preachers, I will just tell them now that I don't even want to hold a meeting for any bunch of brethren who think any negro is a better preacher than I am!"[30] Earlier in his article, Wallace remarked that some women in the church forgot their dignity and "lower[ed] themselves" by shaking hands with Black preachers following their sermons. Drawing on the values of the great chain of being, Wallace positioned himself and other White preachers on a plane far above the one occupied by Black preachers. He went on to criticize Hogan for mixing in company with White people and for making overtures toward social equality. He also condemned a "negro man" working at an orphans' home in Combes, Texas, for moving toward social equality and the White brethren who encouraged him in his pursuits. These specific examples, as well as the tenor of the entire article, reveal Wallace's belief in Black inferiority and White supremacy.

Consistent with his endorsement of Black inferiority, Wallace advanced numerous racial stereotypes. Scientific racism promoted the notion of Black intellectual inferiority, and Wallace seemed to adopt

---

[28] *The Christian Journal* 21, no. 2 (1980).
[29] Wallace, "Negro Meetings for White People."
[30] Wallace, "Negro Meetings for White People."

this notion when he chastised White women for shaking hands with Black preachers "just because a negro has learned enough about the gospel to preach it to his race."[31] His words supported Black intellectual inferiority in two ways. First, he implied that Black preachers knew "enough" of the gospel to preach. Black preachers, even highly successful ones, said Wallace, did not understand the entire gospel, but they knew "enough" of the gospel to preach. Second, a Black preacher knew enough of the gospel to preach to "his own race."[32] Wallace suggested that although a Black preacher knew enough of the gospel to convert and exhort other intellectually inferior Black people, that same preacher did not have the intellectual ability or knowledge to fully satisfy a White audience. This article, in fact, criticizes White people for making Black preachers think otherwise.

Wallace, continuing to substantiate racial stereotypes, utilized a suggestive metaphor when describing the reaction of White Christians toward sermons delivered by Black preachers. He denounced White Christians for becoming enamored by the presentations of Black preachers, indicating White preachers could offer the same words with little to no response. Nevertheless, when White congregants heard those same words from Black preachers, "the brethren paw up the ground over it."[33] Earlier in the article, Wallace described "a prominent [White] brother who went wild over the negroes."[34] In other words, as White people listened to Black preachers, they lowered themselves to the intellectual and behavioral level of Black people, even regressing to the supposed savage and bestial state of native Black people. Wallace used the metaphor of a beast pawing the ground as a sign of its enjoyment or satisfaction, suggesting his acceptance of the idea that Black people, in their most natural state, resembled savage beasts of the field.

Finally, Wallace espoused one of the most common racial stereotypes levied at Black men. As he commended the segregationist

---

[31] Wallace, "Negro Meetings for White People."
[32] Wallace, "Negro Meetings for White People."
[33] Wallace, "Negro Meetings for White People."
[34] Wallace, "Negro Meetings for White People."

behavior of Hardeman, who refused to shake hands with Black people at his meetings, he relayed the story of a "prominent brother in the church" who showed social courtesies to Black people until, one day, a Black man asked the prominent White Christian if he might marry his daughter. Wallace wrote, "That gave the brother a jolt and he changed his attitude!" Scientific racism endorsed the idea that Black men and women, without the guidance and instruction of presumed higher-order human beings, would regress to their supposed bestial and sexually aggressive natures. The 1915 blockbuster film directed by D. W. Griffith, *Birth of a Nation* (based on the novel *The Clansmen* by Thomas Dixon Jr.), for example, tells the fictional story of a savage Black man who kidnaps a White woman to rape her. Eventually, the valiant Knights of the Ku Klux Klan ride in to save the day by rescuing the damsel in distress, reinforcing White supremacy across the land. Wallace stoked the fears of many White fathers of his era—fears that greater contact between White and Black Americans would result in Black men stealing (and perhaps raping) their White daughters. Ironically, during the period of American slavery untold numbers of White men raped Black female slaves and had "children of the plantation," a euphemism given to describe the thousands of offspring born to slave women after they were raped by their White masters.[35]

Consistent with the racial hierarchy created by scientists and theologians in earlier centuries, White racists in the twentieth century mandated that Blacks stay in their preordained place in society. Their place, of course, relegated them far below White citizens and offered them inferior living conditions, jobs, education, and opportunities. Throughout his article, Wallace emphasized the necessity of Christians staying in their places. He exhorted White Christians to abandon their fascination with Black preachers, he complained of

---

[35] See Elizabeth L. Jemison, "Gendering the History of Race and Religion," in *The Oxford Handbook of Religion and Race in American History*, ed. Kathryn Gin Lum and Paul Harvey (Oxford University Press, 2018), 89–90; Jennifer Graber, "Religion and Racial Violence in the Nineteenth Century," in *The Oxford Handbook of Religion and Race in American History*, 387–402.

White and Black citizens working for social equality, and he praised Keeble and Luke Miller (another Black Church of Christ preacher) for staying in their places.

After Wallace's article appeared in March 1941, Keeble wrote him a personal letter, thanking Wallace for his "instructive and encouraging article," and Wallace published that letter in an April 1941 issue of the *Bible Banner*, along with his reply to Keeble.[36] (That letter, along with Wallace's commentary, may be found in Appendix B in the back of this book.) In his response to Keeble, Wallace wrote, "This letter is characteristic of the humility of M. Keeble. It is the reason why he is the greatest colored preacher that has ever lived." He went on to praise Keeble and Miller for their "meekness and humility." Finally, he wrote, "They [Keeble and Miller] know their place and stay in it, even when some white brethren try to take them out of it."[37] Wallace, like so many other White Americans from his era, adhered to and protected a rigid and racially defined caste system, and this article clearly provides evidence that this system provided racial organization to Churches of Christ in the twentieth century.

One of the most damaging aspects of Wallace's article is the degree to which he tied his racism to Christian identity. He described the sleeping arrangement of Hogan and Rice as "an infringement on the Jim Crow law" and "a violation of Christianity itself."[38] Seemingly unaware of the ways in which his racist ideology originated from his cultural context, Wallace believed that when a Black and White man shared a bedroom, their actions transgressed the laws of God. The racism of American culture (especially the culture of the American South) had become so intertwined with White Christianity that it became difficult

---

[36] The racial ideology of Keeble is beyond the scope of this chapter; nevertheless, one should understand that Keeble passively acquiesced to White racism throughout his ministerial career. Strong evidence suggests Keeble adopted his posture intentionally and for the purpose of raising money for Nashville Christian Institute, the school he led for Black students within Churches of Christ. For more on Keeble, see Edward J. Robinson, *Show Us How You Do It: Marshall Keeble and the Rise of Black Churches of Christ in the United States* (University of Alabama Press, 2008); Crawford, *Shattering the Illusion*, 75–81.

[37] Foy Wallace, "From M. Keeble," *Bible Banner* 3, no. 9 (Apr. 1941): 5.

[38] Wallace, "Negro Meetings for White People."

for White Christians to determine where religion ended and culture began. Robert P. Jones's sobering and informative 2020 book, *White Too Long: The Legacy of White Supremacy in American Christianity*, begins to tell the story of this devastating union between racism and American Christianity.[39]

Summarizing the racial legacy of Wallace, Noble Patterson and Terry Gardner wrote:

> By definition most southern white members of churches of Christ would be considered racist in retrospect. To suggest that Foy E. Wallace, Jr., was somehow worse, different, or unique in relation to the majority of his brethren would be unfair. This is not to defend any thing [*sic*] that Foy E. Wallace, Jr., taught that was wrong. With the passing of years, Wallace's attitude regarding race changed. In Wallace's later years he held meetings for mixed, non-segregated congregations in Detroit and other cities . . . Such were the times in 1941.[40]

Certainly, Patterson and Gardner are correct: the attitude of Wallace toward Black people in the 1940s mirrored the thoughts and behaviors of many (perhaps most) other White Americans living in the mid-twentieth century. Nevertheless, as they claimed, this reality did not excuse Wallace's racist behavior.

This chapter intends to highlight a common mindset among White Church of Christ members in the mid-twentieth century. Despite his blatantly racist ideals, Wallace stood among the upper echelon of leaders within his denomination, and when he passed away, denominational journals published special commemorative issues to his memory. Wallace held the respect of his peers, and his racial ideology likely resonated with theirs.

---

[39] Robert P. Jones, *White Too Long: The Legacy of White Supremacy in American Christianity* (Simon & Schuster, 2020).

[40] Patterson and Gardner, *Foy E. Wallace, Jr.*, 65.

One reason contemporary historians cannot excuse Wallace for his racist behavior is because some of his contemporaries did challenge the racist status quo. Carl Spain, Walter Burch, John Allen Chalk, Dwain Evans, and Bud Stumbaugh also lived in the racist climate of twentieth-century Churches of Christ. While others remained silent and refused to challenge the racism of their era, these men broke the silence and demanded change.

The Deaf

Writing in 1909, W. T. Moore, nineteenth- and twentieth-century preacher, educator, and historian of the Stone–Campbell Movement, wrote, "The Disciples of Christ do not have bishops, but they have editors."[1] Lacking a denominational governing body, Churches of Christ (another major stream of the Stone–Campbell Movement) found cohesion and identity maintenance and established theological orthodoxy through less formal structures, including denominational journals.

Throughout most of their history, editors of journals offered an outsized measure of influence for Churches of Christ. Leading up to and during the Civil War, Alexander Campbell guided his Christian movement on the issue of slavery through a series of articles in his *Millennial Harbinger*.[2] In the mid-1930s, Foy E. Wallace Jr. strived to

---

[1] William Moore, *A Comprehensive History of the Disciples of Christ* (Fleming H. Revell, 1909), 12.

[2] Alexander Campbell, "Our Position to American Slavery," *Millennial Harbinger* (Feb. 1845): 50–53. The series continued in the *Millennial Harbinger* in eight parts throughout 1845.

purge premillennialists from Churches of Christ by castigating them from the pages of his *Gospel Guardian* and *Bible Banner*. In fact, Wallace established *The Gospel Guardian* for the express purpose of ridding the denomination of premillennialists.[3]

Throughout the twentieth century, numerous White denominational editors helped to guide Churches of Christ through theological and ecclesial controversies, including dissention centering on race. Two specific White denominational leaders, due largely to their positions of power and influence, stand out among the rest. Reuel Gordon Lemmons edited the *Firm Foundation*, a leading Church of Christ periodical, for nearly three decades in the middle of the twentieth century. Benton Cordell Goodpasture occupied the same role for the *Gospel Advocate*, perhaps the most influential journal for twentieth-century Churches of Christ, from 1939 until his death in 1977. These two White men, from their perches of power, largely ignored the racial revolution in the United States even though they occupied significant positions of influence during the era of Rosa Parks, *Brown v. Board of Education*, Bloody Sunday, the March on Washington, and Martin Luther King Jr. As buses screeched to a halt in Montgomery and as King cast his vision for a dream of a beloved community in Washington, DC, Lemmons and Goodpasture remained deaf to the racial injustice in the United States and in the denomination they led.

Reuel Gordon Lemmons (1908–89)

Born on July 12, 1912, to W. W. and Lucy Lemmons in Pocahontas, Arkansas, Lemmons spent the lion's share of his life as a minister and editor within Churches of Christ. In 1935, he graduated from Abilene Christian College, an institution that would award him an honorary doctorate in 1974. Immediately following his graduation, Lemmons began preaching in various Southern towns, including Tipton, Oklahoma, and Cleburne, Texas. Beginning in 1955, Lemmons edited the *Firm*

---

[3] For a thorough look at Wallace's thoughts on premillennialism, see Foy Wallace, *Modern Millennial Theories Exposed* (Roy E. Cogdill, 1945).

Foundation, and he held this post until 1983. He also served as the founding editor of *Image* from 1985 until his death in 1989. During his life, Lemmons supported worldwide missions, especially in Africa, and in 1948, he helped establish Southwestern Christian College, the only predominantly Black college within Churches of Christ.

Unquestionably, Lemmons's position as editor of the *Firm Foundation* provided the primary platform for his leadership within the denomination. The journal, second in importance only to the *Gospel Advocate* in terms of its influence on twentieth-century Churches of Christ, provided Lemmons a voice that carried into thousands of homes each week. During his tenure as editor, Churches of Christ grew at an unprecedented rate, especially across the South. As the denomination grew, so did Lemmons's influence. Despite his willingness to engage numerous controversial topics (the role of the Holy Spirit, religious legalism, the social gospel, gambling, the sale of liquor, the theory of evolution, and the Vietnam War) during his time as editor of *Firm Foundation*, Lemmons hardly mentioned race, racism, segregation, or the civil rights movement at all. When he did address these topics, he consistently criticized civil rights activists or downplayed the presence of racism within Churches of Christ.[4] In other words, Lemmons remained deaf to the sounds of racial revolution around him.

Unlike Wallace, who left behind stunning racist comments for subsequent generations to examine, Lemmons's racial perspectives come to present generations most audibly through his silence. In an undated article found among his manuscript collection at the Abilene Christian University Center for Restoration Studies, Lemmons wrote of the many castes existent within the world and the church. In the lengthy article, he did mention race twice, but only in passing. He wrote, "Bigots preach white supremacy," and later in the article, he added, "It is difficult to rise above racial prejudice."[5] These two brief mentions receive

---

[4] Wes Crawford, "Lemmons, Reuel Gordon (1912–1989)," in *The Encyclopedia of the Stone–Campbell Movement*, ed. Douglas A. Foster, Paul M. Blowers, Anthony L. Dunnavant, and D. Newell Williams (Eerdmans, 2004), 469.

[5] Reuel Lemmons, "Class Consciousness," Articles by Lemmons, Box 2, Reuel Gordon Lemmons Papers, Center for Restoration Studies, Abilene Christian University.

no commentary, and they come in long lists of other problems. He did, however, contribute pages of material to other castes created between elders and church members, between old and young, between educated and uneducated, and between those with money and those without. Evidence suggests Lemmons did not believe racial castes challenged the United States as severely as generational and educational gaps.

In 1961, Lemmons wrote a sermon titled "Christianity in Perilous Times."[6] He used the sermon to rehearse the long history of the church from the first century to his own era, suggesting the church in 1961 faced its most dangerous obstacles yet. He wrote of the potential of nuclear annihilation. He mentioned the threats posed by Communism and Catholicism (reflecting the sectarianism of mid-twentieth-century Churches of Christ). Instead of dwelling solely on the challenges of his age, he also complimented his denomination for thriving in such a difficult time. He called attention to the many new congregations established, the new buildings built, and the new missionaries sent. Shockingly absent in this article discussing the numerous obstacles standing in the way of American Christian progress is any acknowledgement of the racial unrest in the United States in 1961! By 1961, *Brown v. Board of Education* had already sent shockwaves through the education system in the United States. By 1961, Rosa Parks had already sat in the front seat of a bus in Montgomery, Alabama, thus "violating" the racial status quo in the South and drawing the attention of the entire nation. By 1961, the Little Rock Nine had been escorted through a blockade created by the Arkansas National Guard and into Central High School, flanked by US soldiers. By 1961, four Black students from North Carolina A&T State University had refused to vacate their seats at the F. W. Woolworth lunch counter, thereby instigating the national sit-in movement. By 1961, Ruby Bridges, a six-year-old Black girl, had been escorted into William Frantz Elementary School in New Orleans by armed federal marshals. By 1961, the freedom rides had already begun

---

[6] Reuel Lemmons, "Christianity in Perilous Times," Manuscripts, Box 10, Reuel Gordon Lemmons Papers, Center for Restoration Studies, Abilene Christian University.

across the southern United States. Despite the incredible noise created by the swelling racial revolution, Lemmons remained deaf. When listing example after example of the "perilous times" in the United States during the 1960s, he failed to even mention the racial unrest that had dominated national headlines for the past seven years.

Lemmons rarely addressed events associated with the civil rights movement, and when he did break his silence, his comments reflected the perspective of one who had enjoyed White privilege his entire life. He proved himself unable or unwilling to grasp the root causes of protest. In an article written in January 1968 titled "The Long Hot Summer," Lemmons reacted to the more than 150 race riots that erupted across the United States in the summer of 1967. He laid the blame for those events on moral decay rather than racial prejudice. He wrote, "Some contend that these are the acts of a downtrodden element of society struggling for its fair share of effluency [*sic*]. We deny it. They are, rather, the signs of a decaying and dying society."[7] He continued, "The abandonment of moral principles and the exultation [*sic*] of every vice have wrecked nations before."[8] As examples of the abandonment of moral principles, Lemmons named the immodesty of women and pornography. He argued that the moral decay of the nation led God to repay Americans for their wickedness, writing, "When a nation turns away from God, and rejects eternal verities of moral conduct, the Sodomitish [*sic*] atmosphere soon manifests itself. And even the fire that burns out city blocks and the violence that runs human blood down the gutters is, in a way, sent from heaven."[9] Lacking from Lemmons's article is any awareness of the centuries of hardship, discrimination, violence, and murder endured by Black Americans at the hands of their White counterparts. He mocked those who would blame the events of the long and hot summer on poverty and racial discrimination. Finally, characteristic of so many other White American leaders of his time, Lemmons wrote,

---

[7] Reuel Lemmons, "The Long Hot Summer," *Firm Foundation* 85, no. 2 (1968): 18.

[8] Lemmons, "Long Hot Summer."

[9] Lemmons, "Long Hot Summer."

"It is probably true that Communism is behind most of these riots."[10] Much like White Christians of the early twenty-first century seek to discredit civil rights activism because of its association with socialism, atheism, or progressive political movements, White Christians of the mid-twentieth century consistently laid the blame of social unrest at the feet of Communism. White power has made a habit of discrediting Black protest movements by associating them with the boogeyman of the era.

In a September 1968 article, Lemmons expanded on his indictment of Communism by accusing Christians of adopting the Communists' strategy to instigate change in a society. He posited that Communists sought improvement by applying pressure and creating tension. Contrary to that so-called atheistic method, Lemmons urged Christians to change society through conversion.[11] Not unlike other Southern White Christian leaders of his era, including Billy Graham, Lemmons believed conversion to Christianity provided the remedy to any social ill, including racism. In another article, Lemmons echoed other White Christian leaders by suggesting the church should concentrate on converting lost souls rather than getting embroiled in matters related to civil rights.[12]

As late as 1968, Lemmons incredibly declared his belief that no substantive racial problem existed in the church. He wrote, "According to the speeches of some we are a bunch of fanatical racists and all headed for hell. We do not believe that. It simply isn't so."[13] By the time Lemmons wrote this article, some White and Black leaders within Churches of Christ had begun to speak out boldly against segregation and racism within the denomination, and Lemmons certainly had those leaders and their speeches in mind when he wrote, "To hear some of us speak you would think that Christians were the coldest, hardest,

---

[10] Lemmons, "Long Hot Summer."

[11] Reuel Lemmons, "The Moral Crisis in America," *Firm Foundation* 85, no. 36 (1968): 610.

[12] Reuel Lemmons, "Which Way Are We Going?" *Firm Foundation* 85, no. 27 (1968): 418.

[13] Lemmons, "Moral Crisis in America."

cruelest, most bigoted and prejudiced bunch that the Lord ever let live."[14] The article aimed to criticize the strategy of civil rights activists and silence their voices, but Lemmons's words also provided further proof that he did not acknowledge the pervasive presence of racism within mid-twentieth-century Churches of Christ.

When the famed Black evangelist Marshall Keeble died in April 1968, Lemmons (along with many other White denominational leaders) paid tribute to him in print. Coupled with his praise of Keeble's humility, one finds Lemmons's criticism of civil rights activists:

> He traveled—without discrimination—for seventy years among blacks and whites alike, and equally loved by both, preaching the gospel of Peace . . . He never led a riot; he never burned out a block of buildings; he never marched on Washington. But he marched toward heaven from the day he obeyed the gospel, young in life, and following him a great throng of peaceable people—black and white—and arm in arm, in the common bond of true brotherhood are headed that way.[15]

With these words, Lemmons elevated peace as a chief Christian virtue and criticized those who would challenge unjust laws with their activism. He also blindly declared that Keeble never encountered racism within Churches of Christ, even though the Black evangelist regularly spoke to segregated crowds across the South. He wrote, "If he [Keeble] ever knew there were segregation lines he never indicated it. Indeed, because of his life and work there has been an infinitesimally small amount of racial prejudice in the Church of Christ."[16] Lemmons consistently showed his deafness to racism within his denomination.

His most notable words on the topics of racism and discrimination found voice in the spring of 1964. In March, after years of silence on the

---

[14] Lemmons, "Moral Crisis in America."

[15] Reuel Lemmons, "Marshall Keeble," *Firm Foundation* 85, no. 20 (1968): 306.

[16] Lemmons, "Marshall Keeble," 306.

issue, Lemmons declared that the *Firm Foundation* would finally break its silence by printing two articles on the topic of integration—one in favor of desegregation and the other in favor of the racial status quo. Ahead of those two articles, Lemmons offered his own editorial on the subject. (That editorial, titled "The Church and Integration," may be found in Appendix C at the back of this book.) Once again, he displayed his naivete on the topic by comparing Jim Crow segregation to the way in which the apostle Paul "segregated" himself to live with fellow tentmakers Priscilla and Aquila, and the way in which Jesus "segregated" himself from the world when he went to the desert to be alone.[17] Lemmons never acknowledged an awareness that Jim Crow segregation (in contrast to his anemic examples) involved forced, legal, mandated separation of one group of people from another.

In this article, Lemmons also rehearsed the often articulated position of Southern White Evangelicals that racial discrimination represented a social problem, not a moral one. Drawing on the social nature of these issues, he wrote, "Christianity and the church were neither planned in heaven nor commissioned on earth to revolutionize existing governments nor to uproot social structures."[18] Much like contemporary White Christians who accuse civil rights activists of being too political, White Christians from earlier eras accused civil rights activists of distracting the church from its primary mission of saving lost souls, never perceiving the connection between social justice and the gospel.

The section of Lemmons's article that has received the most attention in later decades provides the fullest picture of his view of racial discrimination in the church. That paragraph is quoted here in its entirety:

> We do not believe that segregation has ever been a problem
> with the Lord's church. In my lifetime I remember only one

---

[17] Reuel Lemmons, "The Church and Integration," *Firm Foundation* 81, no. 13 (1964): 194.

[18] Lemmons, "Church and Integration."

man, in my early childhood, who would deny any human being the right to enter the kingdom of God. I know many thousands of brethren, but only one who was "off" on this point. Name any other religious question under heaven and I believe I can name more brethren who are "off" on it than on this one. It is universally believed among us that "in every nation, those who fear God and work righteousness are acceptable unto him." And certainly if they are acceptable to God they are acceptable to us. Since the day of Pentecost we have had integration in the kingdom of heaven and have believed in it. If that were not true we would not send missionaries to others. We go to men of every race and of every caste and of every vocation with the gospel, offering them the same terms and the same promises and when they accept the gospel we count them our brothers. The kingdom of heaven is the most completely integrated institution we know, and all the brethren accept all the brethren as brethren. We have never had a problem here.[19]

One hardly knows how to respond to such words. Churches of Christ in 1964 remained completely segregated. Most Church of Christ colleges were only beginning to desegregate (over a decade after the Supreme Court mandated the desegregation of schools in *Brown v. Board of Education*). Regardless of these culturally and ecclesiastically mandated divisions, one of the most prominent denominational leaders wrote, "We have never had a problem here." Lemmons's argument rested on his view that Jim Crow segregation fit into the same category as Paul's decision to live with Aquila and Priscilla and Jesus's decision to separate himself from the world to pray to God alone in the wilderness. Such shortsightedness (or racism) kept him from seeing the full implications of mandated segregation based on the color of one's skin.

---

[19] Lemmons, "Church and Integration."

Lemmons's article ended with a plea for Christians to listen to both sides of the argument. Assuming the role of a pastoral denominational leader, he wrote, "Any problem regarding human rights has two sides and the ignoring of either side will bring nothing but heartache."[20] Lemmons attempted to take the middle-ground position on this issue, but he failed to recognize that some issues do not have two acceptable positions. Some actions are unequivocally wrong and should be labeled as such. Surely, he would not encourage his readers to listen politely to the two sides of debate centered on Hitler's extermination of the Jews; yet, he asserted two acceptable positions existed regarding racial segregation in the United States.

Much like twenty-first-century church leaders and not unlike Alexander Campbell's comments about slavery in the mid-nineteenth century, Lemmons valued peace above most other virtues. Also like contemporary and former ecclesial leaders, he understood peace as the absence of conflict. Peace from a biblical point of view, however, occurs when the world exists as God intends, not when conflict is avoided.[21] History has proven that true peace often transpires only on the other side of conflict, when God's people willingly and intentionally confront unjust systems and immoral laws. Lemmons remained unwilling or unable to seek true peace for Churches of Christ in the tumultuous days of the civil rights movement perhaps because he refused to hear the screams for justice coming from his Black brothers and sisters.

Benton Cordell Goodpasture (1895–1977)

The life and career of Benton Goodpasture provides ample evidence that Lemmons was not alone in his deafness. Born in 1895 in Overton County, Tennessee, Goodpasture dedicated his entire life to Christian ministry. Following his graduation from David Lipscomb College in 1918 as valedictorian of his class, he entered full-time ministry, serving

---

[20] Lemmons, "Church and Integration."

[21] See Joseph P. Healey, "Peace, Old Testament," in *The Anchor Bible Dictionary*, vol. 5: *O–Sh*, ed. David Noel Freedman (Doubleday, 1992), 206–7; William Klassen, "Peace, New Testament," *The Anchor Bible Dictionary*, 207–12.

congregations in Tennessee, Georgia, and Alabama. Not long after his graduation, in 1920, he began working as a staff writer for the *Gospel Advocate*, and in 1939, he ascended to the position of editor. For the next thirty-eight years, Goodpasture sat in perhaps the most influential chair within Churches of Christ. John C. Hardin, who wrote his dissertation on the influential editor, wrote, "Goodpasture brought to the editor's chair a dignified manner and a professional persona, characteristics not always associated with Churches of Christ in 1939, but ones increasingly appreciated by church members."[22] Even though Goodpasture guided Churches of Christ for nearly four decades through tumultuous conversations centered on premillennialism, institutionalism, and cooperation (or, more likely, noncooperation) with other Christian denominations, Goodpasture remained deaf and mute on the topics of race, racism, and segregation.

As evidence of his refusal to hear and respond to the noise of racial revolution resounding across the United States in the mid-twentieth century, consider Goodpasture's editorials in the *Gospel Advocate* following key events of the civil rights movement. On May 20, 1954, the United States Supreme Court, in its landmark *Brown v. Board of Education* decision, mandated the desegregation of public schools. Although the decision dominated newspapers, magazines, radio programs, and television shows in the weeks following, the *Gospel Advocate* paid no attention. Goodpasture dedicated the entire issue immediately following the Supreme Court ruling to the topic of the church. Included among several lengthy articles on this topic, Goodpasture included his own article, titled "How to Live in the Church." In that piece, he wrote, "To live in the church one must really live in the church. He must not allow the interests and activities of any other institution to invade the sphere of the church. All his good deeds must be done in the church."[23] Whether Goodpasture intended to describe the dominant Church of

---

[22] John C. Hardin, "Common Cause: B. C. Goodpasture, the *Gospel Advocate*, and Churches of Christ in the Twentieth Century" (PhD diss., Auburn University, 2009), 6.

[23] Benton Goodpasture, "How to Live in the Church," *Gospel Advocate* 96, no. 20 (May 20, 1954): 390.

Christ position toward the civil rights movement is doubtful; nevertheless, his words certainly foreshadowed the denominational response to this racial revolution over the next decade. As the riots, marches, and sit-ins took place throughout the South, most White Church of Christ leaders, including Goodpasture himself, remained inside their buildings, reflecting and writing on other matters.

Emmett Till visited his relatives in Mississippi in the summer of 1955, and on August 28 of that year, in view of his two cousins, William Parker and Simeon Wright, Till was abducted by Roy Bryant and J. W. Milam. The pair kidnapped fourteen-year-old Till, beat him, murdered him, and threw his body into the Tallahatchie River. When authorities recovered the young boy, his body bore witness to the brutality of the crimes committed against him. Against the advice of the funeral home and her relatives, Till's mother, Mamie Till-Mobley, opted for an open-casket funeral. That decision would prove important, because Simeon Booker, a reporter for *Jet* magazine, attended the funeral with his photographer, David Jackson. The latter took a close-up picture of Till's face, which found its way into the September 15, 1955, issue of *Jet* and has become one of the most iconic images in US history.[24] Some suggest Till's death and the national outrage that followed helped spark the civil rights movement. Although Till's story dominated the news cycle for many days and weeks, the Goodpasture-led *Gospel Advocate* never mentioned it or the movement it helped spark. The first issue of the *Gospel Advocate* published following the murder of Till appeared on September 1, and it featured three articles by Goodpasture: "Advocate Circulation Doubles" and two short articles advertising two new regular columns in the journal—"The Pioneer Pulpit" and "What the Religion of Jesus Means to Me." Throughout the next fifteen years, as the civil rights movement demanded the attention of most Americans, the *Gospel Advocate* routinely ignored it, publishing instead articles that discussed the inner workings of the church and biblical interpretation.

---

[24] "Nation Horrified by Murder of Kidnaped Chicago Youth," *Jet* 8, no. 19 (1955): 6–9.

Another seminal event associated with the civil rights movement took place in Montgomery, Alabama, from December 1955 until December 1956. The bus boycott of that city captured headlines across the nation and the world, and it firmly established two individuals as national icons. When Rosa Parks refused to vacate her seat on a Montgomery city bus, she was immediately arrested. Black city leaders (most of them religious leaders) sprang into action, launching a lawsuit against National City Lines, the company that owned the city bus system in Montgomery, and instigating a boycott of the city bus system that lasted 381 days. The recently appointed young preacher of Dexter Avenue Baptist Church, Martin Luther King Jr., assumed leadership of the Montgomery Improvement Association, the organization that coordinated the yearlong boycott. News of the boycott spread far beyond the small Alabama city; the attention of the nation turned toward the regular interviews of King. Finally, in November 1956, the United States Supreme Court upheld the federal district court ruling in *Browder v. Gayle*, declaring bus segregation unconstitutional. Although the boycott pushed King into the world spotlight and although this event garnered national headlines for over a year, Goodpasture failed to acknowledge the enormity of events happening just 280 miles south of his home in Nashville. In the week following the end of the boycott, Goodpasture did not write an editorial at all, and a careful perusal of the journal reveals that not a single article appeared in the *Gospel Advocate* from December 1955 until December 1956 that even mentioned the boycott, race, racism, or segregation.

Those who study the US civil rights movement understand the importance of 1963. In that year, King led a well-publicized campaign in Birmingham, Alabama. Images of police dogs attacking peaceful protesters and police chief Eugene "Bull" Connor barking orders to Birmingham officers captured the imaginations of Americans and produced thousands of volunteers who traveled South to combat Jim Crow segregation. On August 28 of that same year, an estimated 250,000 people gathered in front of the Lincoln Memorial in Washington, DC, to hear speeches from famed civil rights leaders, including King. From the steps of that monument, he delivered perhaps the most iconic speech in US history: "I Have a Dream." Once again in Birmingham, on September 15, 1963, the Ku Klux Klan bombed the 16th Street Baptist Church on a Sunday morning, killing four young Black girls. This event, much like the others from 1963, caught the attention of the entire nation. The frontpage headline of *The Journal News* from White Plains, New York, shouted "Hate-Triggered Church Blast Kills 4 Little Girls." The day following the tragedy, *The Morning Call* from Allentown, Pennsylvania, included the headline "Terror and Death Come with Lesson." The local paper in Odessa, Texas, the *Odessa American*, plastered on the front page "Four Negro Girls Die in Church Bombing." The headline of *The Nashville Tennessean*, where the *Gospel Advocate* was published twice a month and where Goodpasture called home, declared "6 Slain in Birmingham" on its front page and included three separate stories about the Birmingham tragedy.

Not surprisingly, Goodpasture did not publish a single story on any of the pivotal events (many of which centered on American Christian leaders and congregations) of 1963. As the Birmingham campaign moved forward in April and May, he published editorials on the necessity of exposing false teachers in church, vandalizing the church meetinghouse, Paul and the Judaizers, and the biblical authority to give money to orphan homes and colleges.[25] On August 29, just one day following the March on Washington, Goodpasture published an editorial titled "What the Apostles Preached," a reflection on Paul's words from Corinthians 4:5.[26] On September 19, Goodpasture published the first issue of the *Gospel Advocate* following the deadly church bombings in Birmingham. Although nearly every major newspaper in the country addressed that horrific event in detail, Goodpasture did not. Instead, he wrote an article titled "More about 'Recommendations' Concerning

---

[25] Benton Goodpasture, "Here and There," *Gospel Advocate* 105, no. 14 (1963): 210; "Meetinghouse Vandalism," *Gospel Advocate* 105, no. 16 (1963): 242; "Paul and the Judaizers," *Gospel Advocate* 105, no. 17 (1963): 258; "H. Leo Boles on Churches Giving to Orphan Homes and Colleges," *Gospel Advocate* 105, no. 18 (1963): 274.

[26] Benton Goodpasture, "What the Apostles Preached," *Gospel Advocate* 105, no. 35 (1963): 546, 553–54.

the Christian Home in Nashville, Tenn.," and on the following page sits a multipage article written by Batsell Barrett Baxter, another well-recognized leader within the denomination, on the unscriptural basis of using instrumental music in public worship assemblies.[27] The failure of Goodpasture (and others) to even mention the events of 1963 in the *Gospel Advocate* or his inability to see the moral implications of these events for the church bear witness to his deafness.

As one continues to track the dates of important events of the civil rights movement, one notices that Goodpasture remained true to form. On July 9, 1964, just one week after Congress passed the Civil Rights Act, Goodpasture instructed his readers on the unstable character Reuben, son of the patriarch Jacob.[28] Just four days after Bloody Sunday in Selma, Alabama, Goodpasture defended those who characterized the Bible as infallible and errant. In the same article, he criticized those who sought to remain "uncontroversial." Although one might assume Goodpasture finally heard echoes of the gospel as he watched police officers on horseback bludgeon peaceful protesters near the Edmund Pettus Bridge, he, in fact, defined controversy differently. He wrote:

> Jesus was a controversialist. The apostles were controversialists. The Bible is controversial. Christians are commanded "to contend earnestly for the faith which was once for all delivered unto the saints." (Jude 3.) "The faith" is the gospel, the word of God. Once cannot preach the gospel without proclaiming matters that are highly controversial. The facts of the gospel, the death, burial, and resurrection of Jesus, have been and are, highly controversial. So is the "plan of salvation," the work and worship of the church, and the destiny of the good and the bad. The miracles and supernatural are also controversial.[29]

---

[27] Benton Goodpasture, "More About the 'Recommendations' Concerning the Christian Home in Nashville, Tenn.," *Gospel Advocate* 105, no. 38 (1963): 594, 600; Baxter, "Use of Instrumental Music in Worship—Part II," 596–97.

[28] Benton Goodpasture, "Unstable as Water," *Gospel Advocate* 106, no. 28 (1964): 434.

[29] Benton Goodpasture, "Some Modern 'Don'ts,'" *Gospel Advocate* 107, no. 10 (1965): 146–47.

As so many religious leaders in the United States confronted segregation on moral grounds, Goodpasture failed to notice the dissonance between the ethics of Jesus and Jim Crow. He did not recognize or call attention to the controversial nature of Jesus's acceptance of a Samaritan woman or his tendency to love everyone. In this article, Goodpasture could have highlighted the controversial statement of Paul in Galatians 3:28, urging followers of Jesus to recognize no distinctions between male and female, Jew and Gentile, or slave and free. Instead, when defining controversial items, he highlighted miracles, the worship of the church, and the plan of salvation.

The *Gospel Advocate* did finally break its silence on the civil rights movement, but only in a backhanded way. Marshall Keeble died on April 20, 1968. Goodpasture and Keeble shared a longtime relationship. The former had many of Keeble's sermons recorded and published them, along with a short biography, in a 1931 book titled *Biography and Sermons of Marshall Keeble*. Goodpasture performed the wedding ceremony for Keeble and his second wife, Laura Catherine Johnson, in 1934. In fact, Keeble may have been partly responsible for Goodpasture securing the editorship of the *Gospel Advocate*. J. E. Choate, a biographer of Keeble, reported that when Leon McQuiddy was near death and searching for a new editor for the journal, his good friend Keeble recommended Goodpasture. Choate insinuated that Keeble's recommendation may have swayed McQuiddy in that direction.[30] When Keeble passed away, Goodpasture delivered the eulogy in front of a packed Madison Church of Christ, one of the largest congregations among Churches of Christ at the time.

Goodpasture wrote a tribute to Keeble on May 2, 1968, but he dedicated an entire issue to Keeble on July 18. That issue represents the loudest and most articulate voice of Goodpasture and the *Gospel Advocate* on the civil rights movement, even though the issue does not directly address the events from the preceding paragraphs. Instead of speaking about those events, Goodpasture and other writers complimented

---

[30] J. E. Choate, *Roll Jordan Roll: A Biography of Marshall Keeble* (Gospel Advocate Company, 1974), 86–87.

Keeble on the ways in which he refused to follow the tactics of civil rights movement leaders. Goodpasture wrote that Keeble "never listened to alien voices which would array race against race." Goodpasture believed Keeble "too wise to be influenced by those who would exploit his people to foment strife and trouble." Finally, in Goodpasture's final estimation, Keeble "loved peace and always sought to promote it."[31] Surely, Goodpasture loved Keeble and counted him among his friends; nevertheless, one of the things Goodpasture admired most about his friend was Keeble's tendency to stay in his culturally assigned place.

Although he did not write the front-page article of the *Gospel Advocate* on July 18, one should not overlook the fact that Goodpasture accepted "The Memorial to Marshall Keeble" written by Karl W. Pettus and made the decision to feature it on the front page. That article begins:

> In these days when it is difficult to find men of courage to step out and face the storms of social upheaval and political turmoil, men that will face the storms and the winds of change that are blowing all over the world without bending to the forces of evil or the pressures of politically motivated men in the quest for power, it is in these critical days that we have lost a great man, a giant among men, Dr. Marshall Keeble, an aged and honored soldier of the cross, our beloved brother has passed to his reward.[32]

Pettus continued by writing that "no flag was flown at half-mast in his honor," "he wasn't eulogized by our nation's political leaders," and "he never won the coveted *Nobel Prize*." One should note that King died on April 4, 1968, just over two weeks before Keeble. Pettus had the pomp and circumstance of King's passing in mind as he paid tribute to Keeble, contrasting the two Christian leaders. Further contrasting them, he wrote, "He was not called reverend. He was a tolerant man. He was at peace with all men everywhere. He didn't march for school integration,

---

[31] Benton Goodpasture, "The Special Keeble Issue," *Gospel Advocate* 110, no. 29 (1968): 450.

[32] Karl Pettus, "The Memorial to Marshall Keeble," *Gospel Advocate* 110, no. 29 (1968): 449.

but he worked and spent himself for most of his life for Christian education . . . No day or week of mourning has been declared in his memory."[33] After years of ignoring the activities of King and other civil rights leaders, Goodpasture, through the pen of Pettus, allowed his true feelings to be printed in the *Gospel Advocate*. He praised the humility of Keeble and looked on the activism of King with great disdain.

Beneath Goodpasture's critique of King and other civil rights leaders existed the belief that segregation and racism lay far beyond the purview of the church. The Christian, his article from May 20, 1954, declared, "must not allow the interests and activities of any other institution to invade the sphere of the church."[34] Like Lemmons, Goodpasture strived to keep discussions of racism and segregation from the pages of his journal and from the pulpits in Churches of Christ. Also, like Lemmons, Goodpasture did not perceive any real racial problem in the church. Both men held the church, the bride of Christ, in extremely high esteem, believing it far above reproach. As evidence of his high ecclesiology, one should consider his shocking words from 1969. "Slavery," he wrote, "was prevalent in the first century; yet, Christianity did not meet slavery 'head on'; but rather dealt with it indirectly. It has destroyed slavery where it has gone."[35] Far from being complicit in the establishment and perpetuation of chattel slavery, Goodpasture gave the church credit for destroying slavery in every age, and instead of seeing and responding to the racism rampant within Churches of Christ in the mid-twentieth century, he chose to look the other way.

The White editors Lemmons and Goodpasture, perhaps more than any other two individuals, helped create a culture of deafness within mid-twentieth-century Churches of Christ. Certainly, these men knew of Emmett Till, Rosa Parks, the Southern Christian Leadership Conference campaign in Birmingham, the March on Washington, and Bloody Sunday in Selma; nevertheless, they made intentional decisions

---

[33] Pettus, "Memorial to Marshall Keeble."
[34] Goodpasture, "How to Live in the Church."
[35] Benton Goodpasture, "Here and There," *Gospel Advocate* 111, no. 16 (1969): 246.

to censor those culture-altering people and events from the pages of the two most prominent journals associated with Churches of Christ. Their intentional editorial decisions resulted in denominational deafness, thus creating a culture within White Churches of Christ that ignored the systemic impact of racism on the nation and the church and reinforced the illusion of denominational racial harmony.

The Silent

Those standing at the polar ends of long continuums tend to grab the headlines, thereby etching their names in the recorded history of popular culture. Consider some of the most contentious issues of the current era. The phrase "gun control" brings to mind figures such as Ted Nugent, an avid and controversial gun rights activist. One also might think about young Emma Gonzalez, the high school student who burst on the scene as an outspoken activist for gun control in the United States. Abortion lays claim to the title of most polarizing issue of the late twentieth and early twenty-first centuries. The issue conjures images of Evangelical Christians holding picket signs declaring "Abortion is murder." Or, on the other end of the continuum, one might have seen the picture of an activist holding a sign that reads "Keep your Rosaries off My Ovaries." With each of these polarizing debates, the vocal personalities at the edges of the long continuums grab the megaphones and dominate the headlines.

As one considers responses to race among twentieth-century White leaders within Churches of Christ, the names Foy Wallace Jr. and Carl Spain quickly come to mind. One of the foremost leaders in twentieth-century Churches of Christ, Wallace also uttered some of the most racist things ever printed.[1] On the other end of the continuum, Spain stood on the podium during the 1960 Abilene Christian College Lectureship and compared the administration of that school to Communists and Nazis because of their official policy of racial segregation.

Historians remember those standing at the poles, but what about the majority of people who exist in the middle? In reality, most people do not live at the poles; they live in the center—somewhere along that long continuum. This chapter focuses attention on one of those numerous figures who occupied the space in between the two poles. In fact, he made a career of living in the center. Most will not recognize his name because he dedicated his life to staying away from the light that illuminates either pole. And most will not remember his voice because he remained utterly silent.

James Fowler stood in the mold of the Southern White moderate, a figure often criticized by scholars of the US civil rights movement for refusing to choose sides in the struggle for racial equality. The Southern White moderate received praise from White leaders in the mid-twentieth century for providing a calming voice amidst the physical violence and politically charged speeches of the 1950s and 1960s. In his effort to keep the peace and avoid conflict, however, Fowler (along with other Southern White moderates) perpetuated the racist status quo and hindered the progress of civil rights for Black Americans.

Fowler, a longtime preacher and teacher within Churches of Christ, lived on the front lines of the civil rights movement. He occupied the pulpit of Central Church of Christ in Birmingham, Alabama, from 1961 until his death in 1979. Yes, that Birmingham! Martin Luther King Jr.

---

[1] Foy E. Wallace Jr., "Negro Meetings for White People," *Bible Banner* 3, no. 8 (1941); Foy E. Wallace Jr., "From M. Keeble," *Bible Banner* 3, no. 9 (1941).

and the Southern Christian Leadership Conference visited Fowler's Birmingham in 1963 to start one of the most recognized protests against racial injustice in US history. During that campaign, Birmingham police deputies, led by Eugene "Bull" Connor, turned dogs and fire hoses on peaceful protesters for civil rights. Fowler's Birmingham also housed 16th Street Baptist Church, where members of the local chapter of the Ku Klux Klan killed four young Black girls by detonating a bomb in its basement in September 1963. King once called Birmingham "the most thoroughly segregated city in the United States."[2]

Fowler preached each Sunday from the pulpit located inside Central Church of Christ in Birmingham throughout the 1960s; yet, he never joined the protests. But neither did he join the likes of Bull Connor or Governor George Wallace, who lobbied to keep Alabama segregated. Fowler did not support segregation. He, in fact, took the road traveled by countless other Southern White moderates—the middle path. He not only took the middle path; he "baptized" the middle path, describing it as the most holy and New Testament-endorsed option between the two extremes of the violence perpetrated by the Ku Klux Klan on the one hand and the instigated violence brought about by King and other so-called professional agitators on the other hand. By examining the racial attitudes and behaviors of Fowler, one begins to understand better the mind of the Southern White moderate.

Fowler was born on December 17, 1919, in Thorp Spring, Texas, to Thomas G. and Jessie F. Fowler. His parents and both sets of his grandparents staked their membership with Churches of Christ. Fowler's father, Thomas, served as a preacher, teacher, and businessman in Texas. Fowler lived in multiple locations across the state. He graduated from high school in San Antonio in 1937, where he stayed for two years to help his family financially because his father, suffering from depression, found it difficult to maintain a job. As a recent high school graduate, Fowler supported his family for two years before traveling to Abilene

---

[2] Martin Luther King Jr., "Letter from Birmingham Jail," in *Why We Can't Wait* (1964; reprint, Beacon Press, 1986), 87.

to attend Abilene Christian College. Just three years later, in 1942, he graduated with honors with a bachelor's degree in biblical studies, and married Lottie Netterville of Nashville, Tennessee. Lottie began her education at David Lipscomb College in Nashville, and she completed her degree at Abilene Christian College, where she met her husband. The two had four children: one son and three daughters.

Fowler spent his ministerial career in five different congregations. Following his graduation from Abilene Christian College, he and Lottie moved to Temple, Texas, where he preached for the Central Church of Christ from 1942 to 1944. In 1944, Fowler moved to Dallas to work on his master's degree at Southern Methodist University; while there, he worked as a minister at the Shamrock Shores Church of Christ. Upon the completion of his master's degree, he moved his family to College Station, where he ministered from 1946 until 1956. Through an arrangement with the Bible chair at Texas A&M University, he also taught Bible courses. This passion for teaching carried throughout his ministerial career, evidenced by the fact that he often taught classes on church education at various Church of Christ lectureships.

In 1956, the Fowler family moved to Irving. Judy, his youngest daughter, needed special medical treatment for her cerebral palsy. The hospitals in the Dallas–Fort Worth metroplex proved more adept at meeting her medical needs, so the family moved after a ten-year stint in College Station. In Irving, Fowler preached for the South Delaware Church of Christ (a congregation that later merged with the East Side Church of Christ to become South MacArthur Church of Christ). In addition to his preaching responsibilities at South Delaware, Fowler also began working with a television program, *The Way of Life*, a ministry sponsored by the Skillman Avenue congregation. This foray into broadcasting made a lasting impression on Fowler, for he continued to broadcast his ministry through television and radio for the rest of his career. Finally, in 1961, Fowler accepted the preaching minister position at Central Church of Christ in Birmingham and occupied that position until his death in 1979 from a sudden heart attack.

When he arrived at Central, its 650 members made it the largest Church of Christ congregation in town (and one of the largest congregations of any kind in downtown Birmingham). Fowler used his platform at Central to initiate a radio ministry, *Messages for the Master*, which was broadcast to thirty stations in eight states and one foreign country (Belize). This bit of biographical information helps one understand Fowler's context and position within Churches of Christ. He earned advanced degrees, he connected himself with various influential denominational structures, and he occupied a prominent pulpit within the denomination. In other words, Fowler was well-positioned to catalyze denominational change in a critical moment in US history.

Four important moments in Fowler's career exemplify his attitude on the topic of race. The first occurred sometime before 1954, when Fowler worked with the Church of Christ in College Station. Fowler mentioned this event in a letter to Walter Burch in 1967.[3] In that letter, Fowler described this event as having taken place "before the 1954 ruling" (indicating *Brown v. Board of Education*), but he did not report the exact year. A group of Black singers from Southwestern Christian College in Terrell (about 175 miles north of College Station) visited the congregation. After receiving permission from the elders at College Station, Fowler arranged for the group to bring with them a "preacher–student." Fowler also received permission from the elders to invite the "colored" church in Bryan to meet with them on that Sunday afternoon and remain for the Sunday night service. Everyone, Black Christians and White Christians, shared a meal in the annex before the evening service. The Southwestern students led the service, including the singing and the sermon.

The letter provides some interesting information about the days leading up to that event. During a congregational business meeting, someone raised a question concerning the seating arrangement for the event; certain elders of the congregation had grown anxious about

---

[3] James Fowler to Walter Burch (unpublished correspondence, 1967), Fowler Family Papers, 1943–92, Center for Restoration Studies, Abilene Christian University.

the possibility of Black and White Christians sitting together during the service and during the meal. Fowler instructed those attending the business meeting to read James 2:1–4 (in the King James Version, which was customary at the time), with no comment. That text reads:

> My brethren, have not the faith of our Lord Jesus Christ, the Lord of glory, with respect of persons. For if there come unto your assembly a man with a gold ring, in goodly apparel, and there come in also a poor man in vile raiment; And ye have respect to him that weareth the gay clothing, and say unto him, Sit thou here in a good place; and say to the poor, Stand thou there, or sit here under my footstool: Are ye not then partial in yourselves, and are become judges of evil thoughts?

Upon the prompt given by Fowler, most meeting attendees read the text. After a few moments of silence, one of those in attendance suggested that no distinction be made in the seating arrangements. All agreed.

This event highlights a couple of important aspects of Fowler's character. First, one is able to gain a perspective of his boldness. He initiated an integrated worship service (and possibly an integrated meal) in Central Texas before 1954! As a young minister (no older than thirty-five years old), he took the risk of publicly challenging segregation (during the service itself and also during the business meeting that preceded the event). The second aspect of Fowler's character that becomes clear through the lens of this event arises from a comment he made to Burch about it more than thirteen years later. In describing the event, Fowler wrote that he challenged the racial customs of his day "in a quiet and non-crusading way." Obviously, by 1967, Fowler sought to distance himself from the "crusading ways" of the Birmingham civil rights movement protesters of the 1960s.

The second event took place about a decade later in 1963. The year 1963 stands as a landmark moment in Birmingham history. King and the Southern Christian Leadership Conference led a campaign in downtown Birmingham that year (in the shadow of Central Church of Christ). In 1963, members of the Ku Klux Klan bombed the 16th Street Baptist Church, killing four young Black girls. King released his famous "Letter from Birmingham Jail" in 1963. Finally, in 1963, civil rights activists initiated a "kneel-in" movement among Birmingham churches. Their strategy required Black and White protesters to visit White Christian congregations throughout the city on Sunday morning to worship. Obviously, they hoped to challenge the segregation laws (and customs) of Birmingham. Television cameras and news reporters often accompanied the kneel-in activists, ready to share their images with the American public in real time. Anticipating being turned away, the protesters hoped to shine a light on the unjust segregation practices in the South.

Most White congregations in Birmingham, including Central, knew about the planning of the kneel-in movement. In order to prepare for that moment, the elders of Central wrote a policy instructing the congregation how to respond.[4] They advised ushers to allow Black worshipers to enter the building, attend the service, and sit in a segregated area of the sanctuary. By implementing such a strategy, they hoped to avoid a public spectacle.

Unfortunately for them, two would-be Black worshipers arrived on their doorstep on Easter Sunday, one week before they had planned to release the policy to the congregation.[5] The two women were Birmingham residents, and at least one of them considered herself a member of Titusville Church of Christ, a local Black congregation. Caught off guard and unsure how to handle the situation, ushers at the door escorted the two women to a room full of elders, who happened to be gathered for a regularly scheduled meeting that morning before

---

[4] Central Church of Christ Elders, "Policy of the Elders Regarding 'Kneel-in' Demonstrators," Central Church of Christ records, 1961–69, MS #508, Folder I/1, Race Relations, Center for Restoration Studies, Abilene Christian University.

[5] Central Church of Christ Elders, unpublished letter, April 16, 1963, Central Church of Christ records, 1961–69, MS #508, Folder I/1, Race Relations, Center for Restoration Studies, Abilene Christian University.

services. According to a letter written by the Central elders, they met with the two women and spoke for some time.[6] Upon learning that one of the women attended Titusville Church of Christ, the elders "counselled with her regarding her Christian responsibilities for peace and harmony." The elders indicated the two women decided to leave "of their own choice," even though they offered to seat them "if they still thought it was best under the present circumstances."[7]

If the leaders of Central Church of Christ hoped to avoid a public spectacle, they failed miserably in their efforts. The two women reported to local media that they were turned away from worshiping at Central, and the story caught fire. Newspapers from as far away as Chicago printed the story of White Birmingham Christian congregations, including Central Church of Christ, refusing to admit Black worshipers.[8] The Central Church of Christ office began receiving letters from around the country, most from members of Churches of Christ, sharing their disgust. One person wrote, "At least the Presbyterians admitted them."[9] Another wrote, "The church in Birmingham is not the TRUE church."[10] Drawing on the reverence in the denomination for the words of Paul, one disgruntled Christian wrote, "Do you suppose Paul would have refused to preach to someone just because his skin was black?"[11] Still, another person wrote, "I would hate to be at the Gate when you knock and see what St. Peter has to say. Shame on you."[12] In all, the congregation received dozens of such letters, most expressing harsh words of condemnation for the Central elders for their refusal to allow Black worshipers to attend their services.

---

[6] Central Church of Christ Elders, unpublished letter, April 16, 1963.

[7] Central Church of Christ Elders, unpublished letter, April 16, 1963.

[8] "Negroes Attend White Churches," *Chicago Tribune*, April 15, 1963; "2 Churches Admit Negroes, 3 Say No at Birmingham," *Arkansas Democrat-Gazette*, April 14, 1963.

[9] "Criticism Received as a Result of the News Item Re: 'Knee ins,'" Central Church of Christ records, 1961–69, MS #508, Folder I/1, Race Relations, Center for Restoration Studies, Abilene Christian University.

[10] "Criticism Received as a Result of the News Item Re: 'Knee ins.'"

[11] "Criticism Received as a Result of the News Item Re: 'Knee ins.'"

[12] "Criticism Received as a Result of the News Item Re: 'Knee ins.'"

The Center for Restoration Studies at Abilene Christian University, in papers donated by the Palisades Church of Christ (which originated in 1990 from a merger between Central Church of Christ and West End Church of Christ), possesses a detailed account of this event (as recorded by the Central elders). These records include a series of loose-leaf sheets of paper containing a list of names and addresses of those who sent letters to them.[13] Scrupulous in keeping every single correspondence, the elders sent a reply to each individual. The list includes dozens of names, each one crossed off, indicating a reply had been sent. In addition to sending letters to their critics, the elders also sent a letter to members of their own congregation, explaining what had happened from their point of view.[14]

This event dramatically shaped Fowler. He commented on it during a lectureship speech he delivered in 1964 at Pepperdine. He also mentioned it in the letter he wrote to Burch in 1967. In both cases, he condemned the intolerance of those who wrote letters to the church. He labeled the writers of those letters "outsiders" unqualified to comment on the situation in Birmingham. More pointedly, he wrote, "they don't know what living in the Deep South is really like."[15] In this moment, from his position of leadership within the power structure at Central, Fowler modeled the politics of negotiating between various points of view. He sought to pacify the members of Central, justify the actions of the congregation to the outside world, and, ultimately, avoid conflict at all costs.

The third event illuminating Fowler's position on race comes from the speech he delivered during the 1964 Pepperdine Bible Lectures. Reuel Lemmons published a copy of that address, titled "From the Midst of the Crisis," in *Firm Foundation* later in that same year.[16] This

---

[13] "Letters (Integration) Mail," Central Church of Christ records, 1961–69, MS #508, Folder I/2 Desegregation, Center for Restoration Studies, Abilene Christian University.

[14] Central Church of Christ Elders, "Letter to Central Church of Christ Membership," Central Church of Christ records, MS #508, Folder I/1 Desegregation, Center for Restoration Studies, Abilene Christian University.

[15] Fowler to Burch, 1967.

[16] James Fowler, "From the Midst of the Crisis," *Firm Foundation* 81, no. 13 (1964): 199, 205.

sermon represents the most public articulation of Fowler's position on race. In this address, Fowler staked his position (as expected) along the middle path, between the road traveled by violent White supremacists and the one traveled by organized movements, which, according to Fowler, instigated violence. He critiqued the "injustices that have prevailed in the past and still prevail" against Black Americans. He also criticized outside organizers who traveled to Birmingham with the express purpose of creating discord and chaos. He said, "a black man entering a congregation of whites can create an atmosphere as 'politically packed' as a white robed Klansman walking into a negro church."[17]

How could Fowler, and other White moderates, at once criticize violence perpetrated by White terrorists and refuse to engage in activism against it? Like most other White Americans of his time (and perhaps the present time), he viewed racial conflict as a political issue, not a moral issue. He referred to the civil rights movement as a "social revolution." Toward the conclusion of his address, in an effort to contrast the present conflict with weightier matters of the gospel, he said, "Let us not compromise the truth on any moral issue, but let us not by our lack of patience and understanding become more a part of the problem than the answer."[18] According to Fowler, one may accommodate on issues related to race without making a moral compromise.

Most tellingly, Fowler justified his position by appealing to New Testament passages instructing slaves to obey their masters (1 Pet. 2:18; 1 Cor. 7:21; Col. 3:22–23; 1 Tim. 6:1–2; Col. 4:1; Eph. 6:9). Fowler's odd exegetical decisions with these texts led him to draw the conclusion that Paul and other first-century Christian leaders restrained themselves from publicly condemning or acting against a system they believed unjust. Instead, he lauded the first-century leaders for their patience and moderating voices. Finally, Fowler echoed the sentiment of many other White Southerners: "It is my sincere faith that this matter can be and will be worked out by congregations of the south and other sections

---

[17] Fowler, "From the Midst of the Crisis," 199.
[18] Fowler, "From the Midst of the Crisis," 205.

if they are left to work out the problems in the way that seems best for their local situation."[19]

One final moment from Fowler's ministerial career deserves attention: his 1976 Abilene Christian College Lectureship address, "Threats to Our Freedom."[20] The importance of this moment arises not from what Fowler said, but from what he refrained from saying. In the printed manuscript of his address, Fowler recorded examples of threats to Christian freedom modern Christians faced. He mentioned alcohol, drugs, tobacco, and sex. He discussed materialism and money. In a section detailing how prejudice can rob Christians of their freedom, he offered a lengthy illustration of the way in which Christians discriminate against men with long hair. In his manuscript, in a section examining how "brotherhood pressures and politics can enslave us," he used as an example a church in Alabama.[21] A White congregation, fearing the angry (and possibly violent) reaction of their fellow White Christian neighbors, refused to allow their Black brethren access to their baptistry. Fowler ended that example with this statement:

> There are times for both blacks and whites to act with restraint and patience—for expediency's sake; but there are also times when the only right thing to do is to act with boldness and courage even though we may suffer for it. We have come a long, long way in our race relations in the majority of churches, including the one mentioned above, but prejudice still enslaves many on both sides of the color line.[22]

---

[19] Fowler, "From the Midst of the Crisis," 199.

[20] It should also be noted that James Fowler delivered a sermon during the 1967 Abilene Christian College Lectureship titled "Christ in the Community." In that address, he did not encourage the church to engage the civil rights movement, but he did invite individual Christians to engage social problems. He stayed away from the topics of race, racism, and segregation, but he did encourage individual Christians to move from their isolation in order to engage the world. Interestingly, following that sermon, Fowler did not receive another invitation to speak at the Abilene Christian College Lectureship until 1976.

[21] James Fowler, "Threats to Our Freedom," *Abilene Christian College Annual Bible Lectures* (Abilene Christian College Book Store, 1976), 39–40.

[22] Fowler, "Threats to Our Freedom."

Fowler offered a bold and strong illustration! But, alas, Fowler never said these words when he delivered his public address. This illustration exists in his printed manuscript, but he never actually uttered these words from the podium in Abilene.[23] Perhaps he ran out of time and cut his remarks short. Perhaps he overlooked this example in his manuscript. Or perhaps, like many other White moderates of his time, he knew what needed to be said but could not bring himself to say it.

Taken together, what do these four episodes from Fowler's life teach us about his views on race? In a letter dated March 3, 1967, Fowler wrote to Mrs. Sara Ginn. His words to her accurately answer this question. He wrote, "A person can be very sincere in heart and godly in life, and still be enslaved to prevailing cultural traditions and prejudices. Also, there are many 'practical' problems faced by southern communities (and other parts of the nation) that the 'crusader' never sees or seems to understand."[24]

Fowler fit well the definition of the White moderate offered by Carolyn Dupont. She writes of White moderate Evangelicals that "they could wax eloquent about racial equality, but failed to frame the elimination of racial barriers with an urgency or to endorse the measures employed by civil rights activists—marches, direct action, and civil disobedience . . . Moderates often presented themselves as the reasonable middle ground in a struggle waged by extremists on both ends."[25]

Recall Fowler's assessment of the situation in Birmingham in 1963. On the one hand, he criticized the radical and violent White supremacists; on the other hand, he also criticized the civil rights workers, whom he characterized as lawbreakers and instigators of violence. Fowler wore the label "moderate" as a badge of honor and viewed his

---

[23] James Fowler, "Threats to Our Freedom," February 23, 1976, Lectureship and Summit Audio Collection, Center for Restoration Studies, Abilene Christian University, https://digitalcommons.acu.edu/sumlec_audio /5018/.

[24] James Fowler to Sara Gunn, March 3, 1967, Fowler Family Papers, 1943–92, Center for Restoration Studies, Abilene Christian University.

[25] Carolyn Dupont, "White Protestants and the Civil Rights Movement," in *The Oxford Handbook of Religion and Race in American History*, ed. Kathryn Gin Lum and Paul Harvey (Oxford University Press, 2018), 499, 501.

position as most in line with the New Testament principles of peace and harmony.

For American religious historians, Billy Graham represented the quintessential example of the White moderate Evangelical. Not unlike Fowler, Graham resisted the extreme poles on the long continuum. On the one hand, Graham has been characterized as a champion in race relations by some who point to his practice of removing the ropes separating Black and White attendees at his revivals.[26] On the other hand, sometimes Graham allowed the segregated seating arrangements to persist. Additionally, even though he and King often spoke well of each other, Graham criticized King and other civil rights activists for their strategies, which (even though nonviolent) often led to violence by White Americans.[27] When invited to attend the 1963 March on Washington event, Graham declined for fear of being associated with any protesters who might endorse or tolerate violence.[28]

In addition to standing in the middle, White moderate Evangelicals centered their strategy on gradualism. In his letter to Walter Burch, Fowler wrote, "One thing of which I am convinced is that 'gradualism' is our only approach."[29] In his address at the 1964 Pepperdine lectures, he said, "It is my sincere faith that this matter can be and will be worked out by congregations of the south and other sections if they are left to work out their problems in the way that seems best for their local situation."[30]

Finally, Graham and other White moderates (including Fowler) believed the only reasonable cure for racism lay in personal conversion. Graham more than once commented: "It has to come from the hearts of people. That's the answer to the race problem."[31] Although White moderates may have agreed on the unjust nature of segregation,

---

[26] Dupont, "White Protestants and the Civil Rights Movement," 500.

[27] Steven P. Miller, *Billy Graham and the Rise of the Republican South* (University of Pennsylvania Press, 2009), 25.

[28] Dupont, "White Protestants and the Civil Rights Movement," 500–501.

[29] Fowler to Burch, 1967.

[30] Fowler, "From the Midst of the Crisis," 199.

[31] Randall J. Stephens, "'It Has to Come from the Hearts of People': Evangelicals, Fundamentalists, Race, and the 1964 Civil Rights Act," *Journal of American Studies* 50, no. 3 (2016): 559–85.

they disagreed with those who asserted public pressure on politicians, congregations, and businesses to immediately change laws and customs. Instead, they sought to change the hearts of racists in the United States by converting them to Christ. A growing church, then, would conceivably reduce the number of racists in the United States. Dupont, responding to the view that Southern White Christians would eventually persuade all racists to turn from their evil ways, writes, "In fact, in the very region of the country where the vast majority of the populace claimed to have experienced personal salvation, racial oppression flourished most overtly and resisted destruction most fiercely."[32]

Fowler's story offers more than a picture of one isolated Southern Christian minister making his way in the turbulent years of the civil rights movement. His story illumines the path taken by many (if not most) White moderate church leaders in the 1950s and 1960s. Ideologically, they appeared more progressive than many of their White peers, but methodologically or strategically, they acted as impotent as the common White Southerner. In his famous "Letter from Birmingham Jail," King wrote:

> I have almost reached the regrettable conclusion that the Negro's great stumbling block in his stride toward freedom is not the White Citizens' Council or the Ku Klux Klanner, but the white moderate, who is more devoted to 'order' than to justice; who prefers a negative peace which is the absence of tension to a positive peace which is the presence of justice; who constantly says: 'I agree with you in the goal you seek, but I cannot agree with your methods of direct action'; who paternalistically believes he can set the timetable for another man's freedom; who lives by a mystical concept of time and who constantly advises the Negro to wait for a 'more convenient season.' Shallow understanding from people of good will is more frustrating than absolute misunderstanding from

---

[32] Dupont, "White Protestants and the Civil Rights Movement," 501.

people of ill will. Lukewarm acceptance is much more bewil-
dering than outright rejection.[33]

One wonders what might have happened if Fowler had taken a different path. What would have happened if Fowler had allowed his bold
actions in 1954 as a thirty-five-year-old minister in College Station to
set the trajectory of his life? Perhaps he would have been fired and
oppressed like other courageous Southern White ministers who dared
to speak out against racism and segregation.[34] Perhaps he never again
would have spoken at a Church of Christ lectureship. Perhaps he never
would have delivered his 1964 speech, "From the Midst of the Crisis."
Or maybe he would have helped steer a congregation in the heart of
the storm through the midst of that crisis as a harbinger of hope and
reconciliation, rather than one doomed to engage in damage control
after a failed attempt to quietly avoid a public spectacle during the 1963
Birmingham kneel-in campaign. A close examination of James Fowler's
life and legacy sounds this trumpet once more. The White moderate
often champions the causes of peace, tranquility, and the path of least
resistance at moments when our world desperately needs action, confrontation, and prophetic leadership. When the world needs bold and
vocal leadership, the White moderate offers only silence.

---

[33] Martin Luther King Jr., "Letter from Birmingham Jail," in *Blessed are the Peacemakers: Martin Luther King Jr., Eight White Religious Leaders, and the "Letter from Birmingham Jail,"* ed. S. Jonathan Bass (Louisiana State University Press, 2001), 246.

[34] See Elaine Allen Lechtreck, *Southern White Ministers and the Civil Rights Movement* (University Press of Mississippi, 2018) for an in-depth look at the persecution endured by Southern White preachers who dared speak against racism during the US civil rights movement.

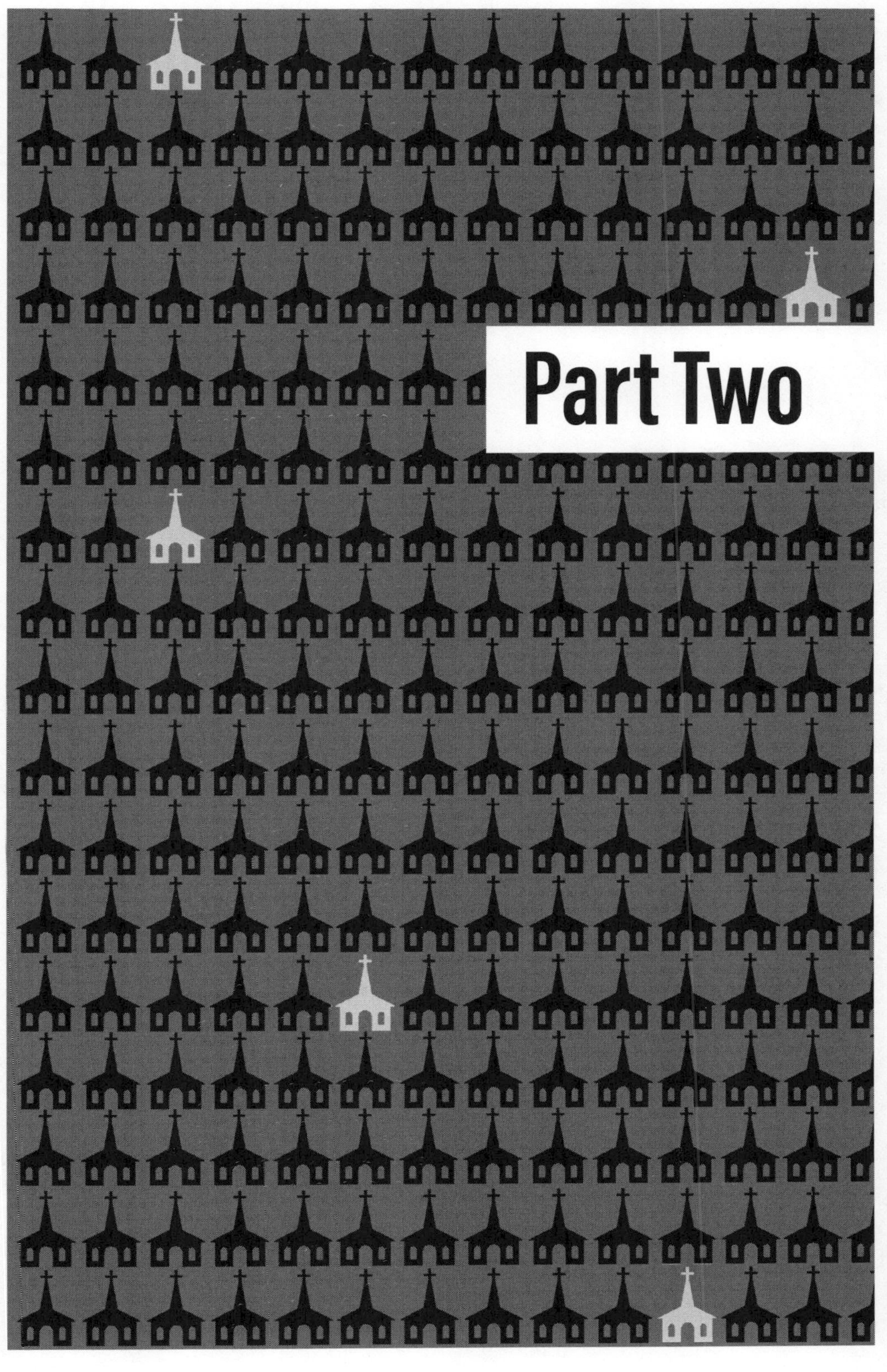

Part Two

The Speech

Churches of Christ comprise a US-born Christian denomination with a domestic membership totaling just over one million people, most of those existing primarily in the Southern United States. More specifically, most members of the denomination live within a one-hundred-mile band stretching from Nashville, Tennessee, to Abilene, Texas. Caucasians make up the vast majority of Churches of Christ membership, while Blacks represent close to 14 percent of denominational members.[1]

Like most other predominantly White Southern denominations, Churches of Christ have poorly addressed racism within their ranks. At the turn of the twentieth century, as Churches of Christ formally separated from Disciples of Christ (largely along regional lines), leaders and members of Churches of Christ joined Lost Cause organizations, such as the Daughters of the Confederacy and Sons of Confederate Veterans, and participated in Lost Cause religious rituals, such as

---

[1] Carl Royster, *Churches of Christ in the United States: 2018 Edition* (21st Century Christian, 2018), 21.

those that regularly took place during Confederate veterans reunions.[2] Additionally, as the civil rights movement spread its influence throughout the South, White members of Churches of Christ, like members of most other Southern predominantly White Christian denominations, either spoke out against the efforts of Martin Luther King Jr. and his peers or ignored their activism altogether.

Most White editors, preachers, educators, and congregational leaders within the denomination (including those discussed in the previous chapters) took an antagonistic posture toward the racial revolution of the mid-twentieth century; yet, a handful of exceptions did exist. Walter Burch, a preacher and marketing expert, organized and led a series of race relations workshops that brought Black and White denominational leaders together to discuss the race problem and outline steps toward a better future. John Allen Chalk, a preacher and host of the internationally broadcast *Herald of Truth* radio program, combated racism in a cutting summer 1968 series wherein he cast racism as one of the three major revolutions being fought in the United States at that time. Two other White Church of Christ leaders, Dwain Evans and Lawrence "Bud" Stumbaugh, also spoke openly and passionately about the racism prevalent within the denomination in the 1960s, and both men, like the scores of other courageous leaders who fought alongside them, paid the price for their bravery. This chapter examines the career and influence of another champion for racial equality: Carl Spain. From his platform as professor at Abilene Christian College, and especially during his 1960 speech at the Abilene Christian College Lectureship, Spain mounted a full frontal attack on the segregated habits of Churches of Christ, including the segregation policy of his employer.

Born in 1917 in Chattanooga, Tennessee, Robert Carl Spain spent his entire life in the South. After attending school in Alabama, he earned undergraduate degrees at both David Lipscomb College in 1936 and Abilene Christian College in 1938. In addition to receiving a

---

[2] See Wes Crawford, "Churches of Christ and Lost Cause Religion: One Southern Denomination's Attempt to Find Identity in Post-Civil War America," *Restoration Quarterly* 64, no. 1 (2022): 1–12.

third bachelor's degree and a master's degree from Southern Methodist University in 1946, he also earned a doctorate in theology from Southwestern Baptist Theological Seminary in Fort Worth in 1963. He joined the Bible faculty at Abilene Christian College in 1954, but not before he taught Bible at Harding College and held the Bible chair at Texas Tech University in Lubbock, Texas. Before Spain began his work in higher education, he served congregations in Texas towns and cities, including Paducah, Handley, Irving, Lubbock, and Houston, and outside of Texas, he served congregations in Auburn, Alabama, and Searcy, Arkansas.

This brief history of Spain's educational and vocational life alerts readers to an important aspect of his identity: Spain was a White Southerner. Unlike so many other White Southerners of his era, however, Spain did not support the racial status quo of his region. He did not espouse White superiority, he did not remain deaf to the voices of Black Americans crying out for help, and he did not remain a silent bystander; rather, he boldly challenged segregation and racism from the most prominent and visible stage available to Church of Christ ministers in the mid-twentieth century.

The most dramatic and effective White challenge to the racial status quo in Churches of Christ came during the 1960 Abilene Christian College Lectureship. (The entire speech may be found in Appendix D at the back of this book.) Those unfamiliar with Churches of Christ should know that lectureships functioned as part revival, part lecture series, and part family reunion. Lacking a general conference or denomination-wide convention, lectureships allowed leaders and laypersons associated with Churches of Christ a venue to gather and hear the most prominent preachers deliver sermons and to network with one another. Lectureships provided space for denominational leaders to define orthodoxy through their sermons and classes, and they were occasions for members and congregations to bind together. Most, but not all, lectureships took place on the campuses of colleges associated with Churches of Christ, including Abilene Christian College, Pepperdine College, and Harding College.

Bill Banowsky (future president of Pepperdine College) referred to the 1960 address as "the most spectacular speech ever delivered in Abilene." To a packed auditorium filled with thousands of denominational members, Spain challenged the segregated status of Church of Christ colleges.[3] He could have attacked racial segregation through many avenues (a radio address, a sermon from a large Church of Christ pulpit, a well-crafted essay, etc.); yet, he chose to attack Jim Crow at the 1960 Abilene Christian College Lectureship. No other platform provided such a wide audience and possibility for rapid change. In Churches of Christ, denominational leaders mediated their theology and set their theological trajectory through these lectureships.

In his sermon, Spain sought to reframe racism and segregation as moral issues, thereby making them fit within the purview of the church. Many of his religious contemporaries sought to distance the church from conversations centering on school desegregation, voting rights, and civil rights activism, claiming those issues belonged on the lips of politicians and judges instead of preachers and church leaders. Spain argued, however, that "worship that is not related to life in social or moral situations is not true worship of God."[4] He said in his address, "We have so defined 'moral' and 'immoral' in our modern times that a covetous idolater and hateful murderer can go to church and be in full fellowship because he doesn't smoke, chew, drink, or dance. These latter things we ought not to do, but we need to expand the borders of our moral realm and condemn certain areas that have been condoned."[5] By reframing segregation as a moral issue (or sin), Spain problematized the gradual solution to segregation and racism advocated by so many White moderates. If segregation constituted sin, the church must challenge it immediately. To use another illustration, if the church found someone practicing adultery against his or her spouse, the church would not say

---

[3] William S. Banowsky, *The Mirror of a Movement: Churches of Christ as Seen through the Abilene Christian College Lectureship* (Christian Publishing, 1965), 385.

[4] Spain, "Modern Challenges to Christian Morals" (1960). Lectureship and Summit Audio Collection, 5199. https://digitalcommons.acu.edu/sumlec_audio/5199.

[5] Spain, "Modern Challenges to Christian Morals."

to the offender, "Eventually, you should quit cheating on your spouse." Rather, leaders of the church would insist the adulterous relationship end immediately.

One of the great contributions of King to the civil rights movement centered on his ability to reframe segregation and prejudice as moral issues. King inherited this idea from Benjamin Mays, a close family friend and president of Morehouse College, where King attended.[6] In addition to the regular conversations King must have had with Mays, the legendary educator also spoke regularly to the students of Morehouse each week during chapel, instilling in them a new understanding of morality. Howard Thurman also influenced King in this way, especially through his book *Jesus and the Disinherited*. King's genius did not arise from his impressive rhetorical ability (many gifted Black preachers graced Christian pulpits across the South). His most significant contribution to the civil rights movement came from his ability to cast segregation as sinful behavior (rather than a political or social issue). Throughout his sermon, Spain echoed this sentiment to his audience in Abilene.

Much like Amos the prophet begins his discourse by attacking distant geographic neighbors of Israel and then slowly moves in concentric circles to challenge his own people, Spain began his address by calling attention to the evil beliefs and practices of Communists in the Soviet Union and Nazis in Germany, but he eventually turned his attention to the "dark chapters in the history of America."[7] His first shot across the bow of his audience came as he said, "Marching under the standard of the god of mammon and bluffing his way with ballots and bullets, the white man put his big white foot on the Negro's neck, quoted the pledge of allegiance to the flag, and piously recited platitudes about all men being born free and equal."[8] He went on to relay his personal

---

[6] See, for example, Freddie C. Colston, "Mays as Mentor to King," in *Walking Integrity: Benjamin Elijah Mays, Mentor to Martin Luther King Jr.*, ed. Lawrence Edward Carter Sr. (Beacon Press, 1998), 197–214; Mark L. Chapman, "'Of One Blood': Mays and the Theology of Race Relations," in *Walking Integrity*, 233–62.

[7] Spain, "Modern Challenges to Christian Morals."

[8] Spain, "Modern Challenges to Christian Morals."

shame in inviting Black people to church, only to have them shunned by his fellow White congregants. He claimed White Christians looked on those Black visitors "like a Jew would have looked upon a 'Samaritan dog.'"[9] Likewise, he shared the experience of an excited group of Black would-be Christians who heard the message of Jesus and sought baptism. The only baptistry available in the vicinity, however, was in a White Church of Christ building. Of that episode, he said:

> The Lord had moved in the hearts of a few white Christians in such a powerful way that they said that their Negro friends would be more than welcome [to use their baptistry]. But the blue-blooded members of the Royal Order of the Master Race, including many members of the Church of Christ, the Baptist, the Methodist, and Presbyterians protested violently.
>
> They preferred death to a fate such as this. Before the baptismal service was over, police came to put a stop to it. Just like the Communists broke up services in Warsaw, Poland, last year. The local paper took up the fight in good old "Democratic" style. Police patrolled the area around the church building. The Lord's church was branded as a communist front organization where whites and Negroes socialized as brothers. The community systematically boycotted the business establishments of some of the Christians for months, nearly causing them to go bankrupt.
>
> I grew up in that community. I saw firsthand the kind of social paranoia that caused the Jews to hate Jesus and nail Him to a tree.[10]

In the days following World War II, nationalism had a considerable influence on US culture and churches, and Churches of Christ followed suit. A movement once dedicated to pacifism stood directly in line with most other Protestant American denominations in their glorification of

---

9 Spain, "Modern Challenges to Christian Morals."
10 Spain, "Modern Challenges to Christian Morals."

the triumphant return of the United States from foreign lands and their denunciation of Communism.[11] In this milieu, Spain said before thousands of people at the Abilene Christian College Lectureship in 1960, "There is little to be gained by preaching against the immoral actions of Communists, unless we as Christians are willing to repent of our own idolatry and murder."[12] Spain not only attacked segregation from the stage of an institution that had not yet complied with *Brown v. Board of Education*, but he also equated racial discrimination with Communism and Nazism. In doing so, he sought to redraw racial boundary lines within the denomination. He went on to say:

> What right have we to talk about the two faces of Khrushchev, when we guard the ballot boxes with guns and pass laws that deny native Americans the right to vote on the basis of their color and social background. Like Khrushchev, many Americans just don't agree with Jesus about His moral code. The ethics of Jesus are foolish to many church goers . . . But when people insist on using the Bible to support an un-Christian system of ethics, one can expect that social revolution will follow, with its usual attending evils.[13]

Reserving his most vehement criticism for Church of Christ colleges, he said, "God forbid that churches of Christ, and schools operated by Christians, shall be the last stronghold of refuge for socially sick people who have Nazi illusions about the Master Race."[14] Of all White-led efforts to challenge White-imposed segregation within Churches of Christ, Spain's effort had the most dramatic effect. Early in 1960, the Abilene Christian College board of trustees, like so many Southern institutions, found itself divided on the issue of segregation and integration.

---

[11] For a look at the decline of pacifism within Churches of Christ, see Richard T. Hughes and James L. Gorman, *Reviving the Ancient Faith: The Story of Churches of Christ in America*, 3rd ed. (Eerdmans, 2024), 109–13.

[12] Spain, "Modern Challenges to Christian Morals."

[13] Spain, "Modern Challenges to Christian Morals."

[14] Spain, "Modern Challenges to Christian Morals."

At that time, the board appointed a special integration committee to examine the issue closely and report back with a recommendation. The committee made long-range plans to desegregate the college, but Spain's speech seems to have increased the speed of those plans. A year after the lectureship, Spain's employer desegregated its graduate school, leading to the desegregation of the entire student body the following year.[15]

One should note an important footnote to this story. During the 1960s, lectureship directors required keynote speakers to deliver advance copies of their speeches to the school administration. Unless Spain ignored that custom or the Abilene Christian College administration did not require him to follow that regular procedure (which seems doubtful, given his topic), key leaders within the administration would have read Spain's words before he delivered them. Knowing what he would say, Abilene Christian College administrators allowed him to speak anyway. This episode stands in stark contrast to an event that took place on the campus of Harding College in 1969. Roosevelt Wells, a well-respected Black minister in Churches of Christ, accepted an invitation to speak during their lectureship that year, but upon receiving an advance copy of his address, "The Case for Black Revolution," the school rescinded his invitation.[16] The fact that Spain's invitation was not rescinded may indicate that the Abilene Christian College administration used his speech to test the waters before they implemented their desegregation policy the following year.

Just months after the 1960 Abilene Christian College Lectureship, *The Christian Chronicle* began publishing letters and editorials on the subject of race relations, which effectively ended the virtual silence on the entire subject among denominational journals.[17] News of the speech,

---

[15] "Effective Next September ACC Desegregates Graduate School," *Christian Chronicle* 18, no. 35 (1961): 1, 6.

[16] Wes Crawford, *Shattering the Illusion: How African American Churches of Christ Moved from Segregation to Independence* (Abilene Christian University Press, 2023), 121. Wells's speech was later published in the July 1970 issue of *Mission*.

[17] "No Hate in His Path," *Christian Chronicle* 17, no. 25 (1960): 2–A; "Readers Tell Own Opinions of Speech on Integration," *Christian Chronicle* 17, no. 25 (1960): 2–A; "Readers Laud Speech," *Christian Chronicle* 17, no. 26 (1960): 2; "Reader Appreciates Policy," *Christian Chronicle* 17, no. 27 (1960): 2; Jim Hawkins, "Dear Editor," *Christian Chronicle* 18, no. 14 (1961): 3.

in fact, spread far beyond Abilene.[18] Spain forced the denomination to acknowledge the reality of the moral revolution at its doorstep. In spite of Spain's ability to end the deafening silence of the denomination on the subject of racial prejudice, however, his efforts at the 1960 lectureship were incapable of changing the racist status quo that had come to dominate Churches of Christ.

Other, more detailed histories of race relationships within Churches of Christ reveal how White and Black denominational factions moved further and further away from each other (both physically and theologically) as the 1960s drew to a close.[19] Despite this dominant trend, a handful of courageous White and Black leaders sought to bridge the ever-increasing racial divide of the denomination. Burch helped organize a series of race relations workshops in Nashville and Atlanta, which were designed to bring key White and Black leaders together to discuss the racism pervading Churches of Christ.[20] He also helped spearhead an effort to publish a special edition of *20th Century Christian* (a denominational magazine) on the topic of race. Evans, Chalk, Stumbaugh, and many other key White leaders of the denomination spoke openly about the racist culture within Churches of Christ during a special meeting in Nashville, and their speeches (and many others) were later published in a special supplemental edition of *The Christian Chronicle*. Following the 1968 race relations workshop in Atlanta, many denominational leaders (White and Black) signed a statement, dedicating themselves

---

[18] See, for example, "At Abilene Church Meet: Admitting Negroes Asked," *San Angelo Standard-Times*, February 24, 1960; Professor Wants to End Discrimination," *The Asheville Times*, February 24, 1960; "Church School is Urged to Admit Negroes," *Tulsa Tribune*, February 24, 1960; "Church of Christ Graduate Study Opening to Negroes Proposed," *Fort Worth Star-Telegram*, February 24, 1960; Church of Christ Colleges Urged to Admit Negroes," *Columbia Daily Tribune*, February 24, 1960; "Asks Colleges Admit Negro Preachers," *Nashville Banner*, February 24, 1960.

[19] See, for example, Crawford, *Shattering the Illusion*; Barclay Key, *Race and Restoration: Churches of Christ and the Black Freedom Struggle* (Louisiana State University Press, 2020).

[20] For an excellent treatment of these conferences, see Doug Foster, "1968 and the Reshaping of the Separation between Black and White Churches of Christ," in *Reconciliation Reconsidered: Advancing the National Conversation on Race in Churches of Christ*, ed. Tanya Smith Brice (Abilene Christian University Press, 2016), 29–41.

to specific habits that would bring about greater racial harmony within Churches of Christ.

One of the most curious observations about Spain's legacy concerns his involvement in these racial reconciliation efforts that took place through the decade of the 1960s. In short, Spain remained virtually invisible. Given his bold claims in 1960 and his influential position among the Abilene Christian College faculty, one would assume his voice would continue to rise above his peers throughout the turbulent years that followed; nevertheless, his voice remained almost silent. He did not attend the small retreat of church leaders who discussed these issues in Nashville in 1966. His name appears on the list of invitees, but he declined the invitation.[21] He did attend the June 1968 race relations workshop in Atlanta, and he did sign his name to the "Statement of Acknowledgement of Racial Prejudice and Proposals for Improving Race Relations in Churches of Christ" document at the workshop, but he did not speak at the event.[22] He did not submit an article for the special issue of *The Christian Chronicle*, but he did submit a short article for the special *20th Century Christian* publication. A newspaper record from the *Redlands Daily Facts* (from Redlands, California) indicates that he delivered an address on February 21, 1966, titled "Undivided in Christ." Although there is no record of the speech, and no strong evidence exists that Spain touched on the topic of race during that address, the newspaper article does mention that he "attracted national attention in 1960 when he challenged Abilene Christian College to open its doors to all races in a blistering attack on the school's admissions policy."[23] Whether or not he tackled the topic of race in that instance, this fact remains: other than his 1960 address, Spain receded to the

---

[21] Walter Burch, "Retreat Invitation List," Walter Burch Collection, Box 8, Re: Race Relations Retreat, Center for Restoration Studies, Abilene Christian University.

[22] Walter Burch, picture of Atlanta race relations workshop attendees, Walter Burch Collection, Box 7, Race Relations Primary #1, Center for Restoration Studies, Abilene Christian University; "Conference on Race Relations," *Mission* 2, no. 3 (1968): 24–25.

[23] "'Undivided in Christ' Campaign: Dr. Carl Spain Talks Tonight in Riverside," *Redlands Daily Facts*, February 21, 1966.

background of the White protest movement in Churches of Christ. Walter Burch wrote a letter to Spain in 1965, asking the professor to critique a sermon he had written on the topic of racism, but no evidence exists that Spain delivered another sermon of his own on race following his 1960 speech.[24] In letters contained in Burch's personal papers, one finds a nickname given to Spain by Burch and a small group of his friends: "Single-Shot Carl."[25] Years later, Burch admitted his shame in using that nickname, but he also expressed his frustration that Spain's prophetic voice against racism remained silent after he descended the stage of the 1960 Abilene Christian College Lectureship.

Spain passed away in 1990. Those curious about his sudden silence do not have the luxury of asking him questions about it directly. Clues do exist, however, that help historians understand his motives. Tim Bench, a chaplain in Abilene, Texas, interviewed Ed Enzor, a longtime communications professor at Abilene Christian University and friend of Spain, during his research on Spain's life. During that interview, Enzor said:

> The impact of his 1960 lectureship speech was seismic in its effect. He infuriated many people, which is reflective of the racial environment of the day, not only in Texas and the deep South, but for some folks even within the churches in those regions. Carl suffered mightily for his views, and I know the amount of venom and long-lasting opposition he endured from a certain few "brethren." But to him, that mattered far less than opening the doors of the university to enrollment of black students, and Carl was willing to pay the price to see justice and equality served.[26]

---

[24] Walter Burch to Carl Spain, 27 October 1965, Walter Burch Collection, Box 8, Race Relations Primary #4 Folder, Center for Restoration Studies, Abilene Christian University.

[25] Walter Burch, "Race Relations Unpublished Correspondence with Bob Douglas," Walter Burch Collection, Box 8, Race Relations Primary #4, Center for Restoration Studies, Abilene Christian University.

[26] Tim Bench, "Carl Spain and the 1960 Abilene Christian College Lectureships," unpublished paper.

Prophets from the Hebrew scriptures, as well as contemporary prophetic preachers, attest to the long suffering that often accompanies challenges to injustice. One may only wonder what kind of persecution Spain and his family endured in the days, weeks, and even years following his 1960 address. He challenged the most prominent and powerful institution of his denomination, and that institution also happened to provide his paycheck. Students of his legacy are safe in assuming the pressure he endured from White power brokers of the denomination forced him into silence.

Even though Spain moved into the shadows of race relations activism, evidence suggests he continued to care deeply about this issue and the people impacted by it the most. He remained a faculty member at Abilene Christian College for many years following his speech, and he helped usher the college through the difficult transition toward desegregation. Once the first Black students began attending the college in the years following his speech, racial tension did not disappear. Terry Childers, the first Black student from Abilene to be admitted to Abilene Christian College, began the process of writing his memoir before his untimely death. Although never published, his manuscript tells an interesting story about Spain from those difficult years. Another Black student and friend of Childers, Charlie Beecham, began dating a White girl. Although the couple initially kept their relationship secret, eventually, the girl's father and brother found out, showed up on campus, and offered to go out with Charlie for a cup of coffee. Once they were alone with him, the pair drove him outside the city and beat Beecham within an inch of his life. Childers writes, "Charlie was left for dead with a clear warning to stay away from the White girl. I went to Hendrick Hospital when I heard about Charlie to check on him. Dr. Carl Spain was there as Charlie talked to the Abilene Police."[27] Far from the limelight and stage of the Abilene Christian College Lectureship, Spain continued to care for and love the Black students that made their way to Abilene.

---

[27] From chapter 4, "Lifetime Decisions," of the unpublished personal memoir of Terry Childers in the possession of his wife, Essie Childers: Terry L. Childers, "My Journey: The Life Story of Terry L. Childers," 2021.

Despite his sudden silence, Spain deserves a privileged seat at the table reserved for the small company of crusaders who challenged segregation and racism in twentieth-century Churches of Christ. Although his public activism did not endure, it certainly had a profound impact on the denomination. In fact, one could argue that his one moment in the spotlight resulted in more systemic change than all other efforts from the 1960s combined.

In 2018, Abilene Christian University established the Carl Spain Center on Race Studies and Spiritual Action, under the leadership of Jerry Taylor. This center stands as a testimony to Spain's prophetic sermon at the lectureship hosted over half of a century ago by Abilene Christian College (now University). From his post as director of the center, Taylor provides racial reconciliation resources to congregations across the country, hosts conferences on this topic from coast to coast, and even invites White and Black ministers to accompany him on periodic bus rides across the South to learn about the history of racism and segregation in our nation. Spain's voice went silent following the 1960 Abilene Christian College Lectureship, but his voice continues to reverberate through the activism of the center that bears his name.

The Conductor

Although most White leaders and members remained silent or antagonistic toward the civil rights movement or any effort to challenge racism or laws promoting segregation in the mid-twentieth century, exceptions to this general rule did exist. To begin with, one should recognize the numerous Black leaders who challenged the racial status quo of Churches of Christ in this era. Fred Gray occupied a central role in the civil rights movement as one of King's most trusted attorneys. Richard Nathaniel Hogan, from the pages of *The Christian Echo*, routinely castigated White denominational leaders for their racist behavior, especially their refusal to allow Black students to attend denominational colleges. Floyd Rose led civil rights efforts in Toledo, Ohio, and Valdosta, Georgia, to such an extent that a White chief of police in Valdosta referred to Rose as "the MLK down here."[1] Franklin Florence maintained a close and personal friendship with Malcolm X

---

[1] Floyd Rose, "Honoring the Late Dr. Martin Luther King, Jr.," *Valdosta Daily Times*, January 14, 2017.

and led a national campaign against Eastman Kodak for its discriminatory hiring practices.[2] The evidence bears witness that numerous Black leaders within Churches of Christ actively participated in the civil rights movement.

Among their White denominational counterparts, most remained silent or even vehemently opposed to the Movement, but a few courageous individuals risked their reputations and their positions to speak out publicly against racism within Churches of Christ. Most studies of White civil rights activists within Churches of Christ center on Abilene Christian College professor Carl Spain (the main subject of Chapter Four).

Certainly, Spain deserves much credit for his legendary speech, but one should acknowledge that other White individuals within Churches of Christ cut against the grain as well. This chapter seeks to bring to the foreground an often unnoticed or completely ignored figure from this era. Although overlooked among civil rights activists, Walter Burch stands without peers among White leaders within Churches of Christ who advanced the agenda for racial equality in the 1960s.

Throughout his adult life, Burch held many vocational positions. He worked as director of development for Abilene Christian College in the early 1960s. After attending graduate school at Columbia University in New York City, he returned to Abilene to help the college in its public relations department, while at the same time working at a local ad agency. In 1967, Burch moved back to New York and started his own company. Throughout his entire adult life, as Burch worked in marketing, public relations, and publishing, he also preached. In fact, Burch became a mainstay and sought-after speaker at Church of Christ meetings and lectureships. Burch's status within the denomination afforded him a privileged place from which to instigate change, and throughout the 1960s, Burch utilized his position to orchestrate a direct attack on racism.

---

[2] R. D. G. Wadhwani, "Kodak, FIGHT, and the Definition of Civil Rights in Rochester, New York: 1966–1967," *The Historian* 60, no. 1 (1997): 59–75.

Three Significant Conferences

As one considers the activism of Burch, three significant conferences and two influential journalistic efforts provide ample proof of his crucial role in changing the trajectory of race relationships within twentieth-century Churches of Christ. Burch initiated three race relations events, one in 1966 and the other two in 1968, which brought together key Black and White leaders of the denomination to confront the issue of racism and to work toward a better future. Likewise, he planned, organized, and edited a special edition journal and wrote an influential essay of his own that created meaningful dialogue on the topics of race and racism within Churches of Christ. This chapter describes each of these efforts in detail, providing proof of Burch's ability to conduct the small symphony of voices crying out for racial equality in the 1960s.

The 1966 Nashville Retreat

In January 1966, Burch helped organize and lead an underground, by-invitation-only meeting of denominational leaders in Nashville, Tennessee. Eighty-three invitations were sent, and at least forty people attended. The retreat took place January 10–11 in a downtown Nashville hotel, and it brought together some of the most influential Black and White leaders of mid-twentieth-century Churches of Christ, including Jimmy Allen (Harding College professor), Franklin Florence (civil rights activist and preacher), Hubert Locke (Detroit civil rights organizer and eventual dean of public affairs at the University of Washington), John Stevens (president of Abilene Christian College), Norvel Young (president of Pepperdine College), and Batsell Barrett Baxter (regularly featured preacher on the nationally televised and radio broadcast program *Herald of Truth*). The invited speakers presented prepared remarks on a variety of issues, including materialism and sectarianism, but the topic of race took center stage.

Behind closed doors and out of the public eye, many of these leaders felt more at ease to discuss controversial topics. In his report of the retreat nearly fifteen years later, Burch indicated that no one publicized the event, no tape recorders were permitted in the room, and as far as he knew, he held the only hard copies of the speech manuscripts.[3] Even though event organizers worked diligently to keep the speeches out of the public eye, apparently some words from the proceedings leaked out from behind closed doors. Stevens remarked to Burch following the retreat that his address on the topic of sectarianism in the church almost "cost me the presidency of Abilene Christian College."[4]

In this semi-private environment, some of the most influential voices within the denomination talked openly and frankly about the historic pattern of racism within Churches of Christ. Florence, for one, expressed his bitterness that White members of the denomination had for so long evaded the racial issue. Burch compared the White church to a bleeding arm, saying that it needed immediate attention. He further employed the analogy with the words, "No one would say to a man with a bleeding arm, 'Just give it more time.'"[5] Burch delivered the final address of the retreat and provided a summary of the most poignant moments. In that final speech, he said, "If the white church does not address this issue, they will present a distorted view of New Testament Christianity to the world."[6] To a room filled with church leaders who viewed the restoration of New Testament Christianity as a paramount aim of the Christian life, Burch's words sounded the alarm to the seriousness of racism in the church.

Toward the conclusion of the meeting, Burch offered a series of recommendations to the attendees. He encouraged the men to arrange meetings with elders and deacons in their home congregations to discuss these issues in greater detail. He admonished college professors and administrators to host similar meetings on their campuses with colleagues and students. He recommended they attend future retreats

---

[3] Walter Burch, "Race Relations Unpublished Correspondence with Bob Douglas," Walter Burch Collection, Box 8, Race Relations Primary #4, Center for Restoration Studies, Abilene Christian University.

[4] Burch, "Race Relations Unpublished Correspondence with Bob Douglas."

[5] Burch, "Race Relations Unpublished Correspondence with Bob Douglas."

[6] Walter Burch, "Come Thou to Faithful Men," Walter Burch Collection, Box 8, Race Relations Primary #5 Folder, Center for Restoration Studies, Abilene Christian University.

and workshops dedicated to exploring this topic further. Finally, he suggested that many of the attendees take it upon themselves to write articles for denominational publications, calling attention to the past and present sin of racism in the church.

From the surviving records of this retreat, students of history learn at least two things relevant to this study. First, Burch stood at the center of this effort. He organized it, presided over it, and offered its final summarizing address.[7] One could accurately refer to him as the "conductor" of this symphony. Second, this retreat marked the first conference on the topic of race ever assembled within Churches of Christ. This event challenged these few pivotal denominational leaders to break their silence on this issue, and some of them did.

The 1968 Race Relations Workshop in Nashville

Two years later, in 1968, a much larger gathering took place at the all-Black Schrader Lane Church of Christ in Nashville—the first of two race relations workshops. In contrast to the secretive nature of the Nashville retreat in 1966, all Churches of Christ in Davidson County, Tennessee, received invitations to this meeting. The five-night event drew crowds of up to seven hundred people, with an average of just under 550 per evening.[8] Lawrence "Bud" Stumbaugh, a White minister who had recently been fired from his post for preaching on the topic of race in Birmingham, Alabama, and Jonesboro, Arkansas, along with David Jones, preaching minister for the Schrader Lane congregation, served as the principal organizers for this event. Nevertheless, Burch remained a key figure involved in the planning and orchestrating of this first race relations workshop.

The Nashville workshop centered around speeches delivered by eleven well-known preachers (five Black and six White). David Jones, Walter Burch, Bud Stumbaugh, James Dennis, and Don Finto each

---

[7] See a letter from Dwain Evans to Walter Burch, thanking him for "shouldering so much of the responsibility" for the retreat. Dwain Evans to Walter Burch, January 20, 1966, Walter Burch Collection, Box 8, Nashville Retreat Folder, Center for Restoration Studies, Abilene Christian University.

[8] "Background of Race Relations Workshop," *Christian Chronicle*, supplemental issue (May 10, 1968): 3.

presented keynote sermons on the topic, and an entire session centered on the statements of six college students from Tennessee A&I State, David Lipscomb College, the University of Tennessee, and Vanderbilt University.[9]

Echoing the sentiments of his Nashville address from 1966, Burch said to the crowd two years later, "The shameful spectre [*sic*] of discrimination against the poor, and the racial injustice implicitly sanctioned by our brotherhood is a disgrace that patently nullifies the claim of Churches of Christ to have restored New Testament Christianity."[10] Once again, in front of hundreds of people, Burch publicly and pointedly challenged the racist practices of the denomination.

Reflecting on the event years later, Burch remembered the disillusionment of the participating college students, stemming from the refusal of so many White church leaders to attend the workshop. Even though White members far outnumbered Black members (then and now), and even though Nashville hosted some of the largest and most influential White congregations of the denomination (then and now), during most evening sessions, Black attendees made up more than 60 percent of the audience. Burch, along with other leaders present at the workshop, surely hoped their passionate pleas against racial injustice would have reached a wider audience. In fact, their words did reach far beyond the auditorium of Schrader Lane Church of Christ. Following Burch's suggestion and under his leadership, transcripts of the race relations workshop speeches were collected and published in a special issue of *The Christian Chronicle*, a leading newspaper within Churches of Christ. During the workshop, attendees donated $1,600 to help defray the cost of the special issue, which reached the public on May 10, 1968.

---

[9] The student presenters were Fred Leon Hill (Tennessee A&I State), Phillip Roseberry (David Lipscomb College), Joseph Tucker (University of Tennessee), Joe Tomlinson (David Lipscomb College), Perry Wallace (Vanderbilt University), and Jim Mayo (unknown college).

[10] Walter Burch, "The Image of the Church," *Christian Chronicle*, supplemental issue (May 10, 1968): 27.

The 1968 Race Relations Workshop in Atlanta

A second race relations workshop took place on June 25–26, 1968, in Atlanta at Simpson Street Church of Christ, the home congregation of Andrew Hairston. In addition to his preaching responsibilities, Hairston made a name for himself as a civil rights activist, eventually passed the bar exam, and became the first Black person elected as Atlanta City Court judge in 1982. Even though Hairston hosted the event, Burch was the true originator and catalyst for the workshop. Burch's archives reveal that he had become "sufficiently tarnished as a 'liberal' who would have no influence getting white church leaders to a race relations conference, so Jimmy Allen was asked to help organize the conference."[11] Allen, a well-respected college professor and dynamic public speaker, seemed a logical choice to advertise the event, for his invitation would attract a wide audience to the workshop.

The first planning meeting for the Atlanta workshop took place in Harlem, New York City, with Burch, Roosevelt Wells, and Eugene Lawton in attendance. Wells and Lawton eventually worked with Allen as the public faces for the event, signing their names to invitation letters and making personal appeals to potential speakers. Adding a bit of institutional authority to the event, Allen sent formal invitations on Harding College letterhead.

One important outcome of this workshop centered on a "Statement of Acknowledgement of Racial Prejudice and Proposals for Improving Race Relations in Churches of Christ," a petition signed by thirty-five of the forty-seven workshop attendees. (That document may be seen in Appendix E of this book.) The petition outlined suggestions for local congregations, colleges, the *Herald of Truth* radio and television program, publishing companies, Christian-owned businesses, and all Christians to bring about better race relationships within Churches of Christ. Signers of the petition agreed to become more vocal in their protests against discriminatory hiring practices, speak courageously

---

[11] Burch, "Race Relations Unpublished Correspondence with Bob Douglas."

against the sin of racial discrimination, increase recruitment of Black students to denominational colleges, and host race relations workshops in local congregations across the United States. In all, the petition included twenty-nine items. Although far-reaching in its aspirations, Burch described the workshop and the petition itself as a "toothless tiger," lamenting the fact that so many White Christian leaders refused to sign their names to the document.[12]

The meeting did, nevertheless, highlight the need for such a workshop. Jim Bill McInteer, business manager for *20th Century Christian* magazine, delivered a speech highlighting the ways in which Church of Christ publications could address the issue of denominational racism. Echoing Reuel Lemmons, McInteer reported that most of the editors he surveyed indicated their belief that no problem existed at all. After McInteer delivered his address, during the question-and-answer portion of the program, a Black attendee asked McInteer if, during his research, he had contacted Richard Nathaniel Hogan, editor of *The Christian Echo*, the only journal within Churches of Christ operated by and aimed toward Black members of the denomination. In response, McInteer indicated he had never heard of *The Christian Echo*, which had been in print since 1902! When McInteer made this comment, Hogan sat just a few feet away. Such ignorance highlighted once again the deep chasm that existed between Black and White constituencies of the denomination and underscored the importance of people like Burch who worked tirelessly to bridge that divide.

Special Issue of 20th Century Christian

In addition to his tireless efforts to plan and organize these three workshops, Burch also orchestrated two important journalistic efforts. Following the Atlanta workshop, Burch once again set in motion a plan to allow Black and White leaders to critique the racist habits of Churches of Christ in printed form. The special issue of *20th Century*

---

[12] Burch, "Race Relations Unpublished Correspondence with Bob Douglas." Among those who refused to sign their names to the petition were Clifton Ganus, John Stevens, Ralph Sweet, and Jim Bill McInteer.

Christian in June 1968 demanded considerable attention as one of Burch's most remarkable publishing feats.

In 1968, *20th Century Christian* bore considerable weight within Churches of Christ. Its editor, M. Norvel Young, offered substantial leadership to the denomination over many decades as both a prominent preacher and college administrator. From 1944 to 1957, Young filled the pulpit at the largest Church of Christ congregation in the world at that time, Broadway Church of Christ in Lubbock, Texas. In 1957, he left Lubbock for Southern California to become president of Pepperdine College. He also contributed significantly to the founding of Lubbock Christian College in 1957. The associate editor of *20th Century Christian*, William S. Banowsky, occupied the Broadway pulpit in 1968, but by that time he already was planning a move to Los Angeles to help Young move Pepperdine to Malibu. Banowsky had already earned a certain level of fame for debating Anson Mount, religion editor for *Playboy* magazine, in 1967 before an audience of three thousand people at the Municipal Auditorium in Lubbock. The debate received national attention and highlighted Banowsky's prodigious rhetorical ability. He would eventually follow in Young's footsteps as president of Pepperdine University, and he later traveled to Norman, Oklahoma, to become president of the University of Oklahoma. Banowsky also displayed tremendous political ambition throughout his adult life, serving as a member of the Republican National Committee for the state of California in 1973–75; working closely with the presidential campaigns of Richard Nixon, Gerald Ford, and Ronald Reagan; and even considering a run for the United States Senate in 1976.[13] This brief biographical sketch of the editors of *20th Century Christian* provides important context for the present study. Young and Banowsky occupied key positions of authority within Churches of Christ, and each had refined the political skills one needs to arise to such places of prominence. Burch convinced these two politically minded power brokers within Churches of Christ to put their reputations on the line by publishing a special

---

[13] John Dreyfuss, "Bill Banowsky: He's a Man at a Crossroads," *Los Angeles Times*, February 18, 1975.

edition of their journal, featuring hard-hitting essays that directly challenged the racist patterns of the denomination.

Burch first proposed the idea to Banowsky in 1967, before the Atlanta workshop even took place. Banowsky supported the idea and dubbed Burch the editor of the special issue. Banowsky also gave strict instructions to Burch and Lawton (coeditor of the special issue and a Black preacher in New York City) to freely explore the biblical teaching on the subject "without deepening the antagonisms between brethren who may honestly disagree with your conclusions."[14] This first set of instructions foreshadowed the ongoing tensions that would surround this special publication. Burch's records of this event indicate that Young and Banowsky consistently aired their reservations and concerns about the articles chosen to appear in the issue. At one point, the editors had to decide whether to include articles written by Black authors, because the journal had never printed such articles before. Fearing serious repercussions, the editors eventually decided to cut Burch's article, believing it too radical for their predominantly White audience. Young worried, especially, about the potential backlash from the Nashville establishment, and there appears to have even been pressure from his own family not to publish the issue. Burch indicates that while he gathered with Young and Lawton for a meeting in New York City weeks before the release of the publication, Young received a last-minute letter from his son, urging his father not to proceed with the publication.[15] In his final estimation, Burch wrote, "It was a miracle the issue was published, given all of its obstacles."[16]

To their credit, Young and Banowsky published the special issue. In a letter from Young to Burch shortly before the release of the issue to the public, Young wrote, "I am sure we can expect a lot of letters about our issue. It will probably reduce our subscriptions by several thousand, but I believe it is needed and I am thankful to have a part in promoting

---

[14] Burch, "Race Relations Unpublished Correspondence with Bob Douglas."

[15] Burch, "Race Relations Unpublished Correspondence with Bob Douglas."

[16] Burch, "Race Relations Unpublished Correspondence with Bob Douglas."

a more Christian attitude and action on the racial problem."[17] The fan mail did arrive, and the subscriptions did decrease, but as a testimony to their resolve and to Burch's dogged determination, the special issue furthered Burch's efforts to break the silence of White members of Churches of Christ on the topic of race.

"Neglecting the Weightier Matters"

As already mentioned, Young and Banowsky rejected the first article Burch submitted for the special issue (although he eventually would submit a different article that would be included in the publication). Burch continued to believe his first article, which he titled "Neglecting the Weightier Matters," deserved a larger audience, so he submitted it to *Firm Foundation*, one of the most influential denominational journals at the time. To his great surprise (Lemmons, editor of the *Firm Foundation*, did not believe a racial problem existed in the church), the journal published his article in June 1968.

In perhaps the clearest articulation of his perspective on race, Burch chastised members of Churches of Christ for refusing to engage "the single most pervasive moral issue of our age."[18] Many White Southerners, including members of Churches of Christ, claimed the church should refrain from engaging questions surrounding race because of its political or social nature. In other words, the church should focus solely on so-called spiritual issues and leave the social and political questions to the government. Responding to this sentiment, Burch called attention to the many ways in which White Churches of Christ became heavily involved in the 1960 presidential election, hoping to keep a Roman Catholic from gaining control of the White House. He also mentioned how actively White Christians within his denomination campaigned against evolution being taught in public school classrooms, their opposition to school-sponsored dances, their fights against legislation that

---

[17] Norvel Young to Walter Burch, July 17, 1968, Walter Burch Collection, Box 8, special issue of *20th Century Christian* on Race Relations and the Controversy that Followed Folder, Center for Restoration Studies, Abilene Christian University.

[18] Walter Burch, "Neglecting the Weightier Matters," *Firm Foundation* 85, no. 24 (1968): 372.

would legalize the sale of alcohol in their counties, and their willingness to join efforts to oppose the legalization of pari-mutuel betting (gambling at racetracks).[19] In other words, Burch openly called out their hypocrisy.

The response to his article came quickly and forcefully. Lemmons, who did not agree with Burch, dedicated the entire next issue of the *Firm Foundation* to articles rebutting his position. Lemmons opened that issue with his own editorial, making the claim that the responses received concerning "Neglecting the Weightier Matters" have "all been one-sided."[20] He concluded his editorial with the claim, "We still believe that racial prejudice is gross in an infinitesimally small part of the body of Christ."[21]

Following the publication of "Neglecting the Weightier Matters" and the issue of *Firm Foundation* that followed, Burch solidified his exile from the inner circle of Churches of Christ preachers. Reminiscing in 1979, Burch said those closest to him always were urging him to use his influence for the cause of racial justice. He wrote, "I did use my influence. Some say I 'used it all up.'"[22]

Conclusion

Most histories of mid-twentieth-century Churches of Christ accurately describe White members of the denomination as either silent or antagonistic toward the civil rights movement. This chapter, however, reminds students of history that exceptions did exist to this general rule, and the list of those exceptions included names other than Carl Spain. Spain surely endured significant backlash for his prophetic words in 1960, and one can understand how such backlash pushed him to the shadows of the protest movement. Nevertheless, that reality makes Burch's decade-long crusade against racism within Churches of Christ that much more remarkable.

---

[19] Burch, "Neglecting the Weightier Matters."

[20] Reuel Lemmons, "Editorial," *Firm Foundation* 85, no. 28 (1968): 434.

[21] Lemmons, "Editorial."

[22] Burch, "Race Relations Unpublished Correspondence with Bob Douglas."

Jeopardizing and forever tarnishing his reputation among White Church of Christ leaders, Burch publicly and vocally attacked the sin of racism within the denomination for many years. He also pulled the most prominent denominational leaders onto the stage with him, thereby conducting a small orchestra for racial justice where there had been virtual silence.

The Herald

The small cadre of White leaders combating the historic patterns of racism within Churches of Christ included a legendary speech to break the silence of the denomination and a conductor to coordinate the multiple voices crying out for racial equality. That small courageous contingent also included a herald. This chapter examines the career and influence of another often ignored champion for racial equality—John Allen Chalk. From his platform as writer and host of the international radio program *Herald of Truth*, Chalk boldly and publicly challenged the racist status quo of Churches of Christ in the late 1960s.

Born in 1937, Chalk served as a prominent young minister within Churches of Christ from 1956 until 1971, when he began his legal career by attending law school at The University of Texas at Austin. As a preacher in Ohio, Tennessee, and Texas, Chalk earned a reputation as an effective and talented communicator, one unwilling to ignore pressing issues confronting the church. These attributes eventually won him the position of writer and host of the international radio program *Herald of Truth.*

During his tenure at *Herald of Truth* (1966–69), the program, which was based in Abilene, Texas, was broadcast internationally to approximately six hundred radio stations and 150 television stations, including NBC and ABC. Financial support for *Herald of Truth* came from two thousand independent Church of Christ congregations, and oversight of the ministry rested with the elders of the Highland Church of Christ, a large congregation in Abilene. Each week, Chalk wrote the manuscript for the show (which essentially consisted of a sermon), read it aloud before the Highland elders for their suggestions and approval, and finally presented the finished address live on the program.[1]

Three American Revolutions

The most notable sermon series delivered by Chalk, and perhaps the best-known series in the history of *Herald of Truth*, found its way into living rooms around the world in the summer of 1968. The thirteen-week series, titled "Three American Revolutions," tackled three major issues confronting Americans in the waning years of the 1960s: crime, race, and sex. Most significant for the present study were the four lessons in Chalk's series pertaining to racism in the United States. Keep in mind the turbulent events that took place in the late 1960s: the Watts riots; Bloody Sunday in Selma, Alabama; the passage of the Voting Rights Act; and Martin Luther King Jr.'s assassination. These events (and many others) served as the backdrop for Chalk's radio address, which offered a stinging critique of the racist behavior of US Christians.

In the first of his lessons, "Hatred is Only Skin Deep," Chalk, much like Carl Spain did in 1960, compared American racism to Hitler's ideology. He said:

---

[1] John Allen Chalk, "Herald of Truth 1966–69: The Turbulent Years" (Friends of ACU Library Lecture, ACU Summit, Abilene, TX, September 21, 2015).

Hitler's justification of Nazi pretensions to Aryan superiority centered on the twin observations that "every animal mates only with a member of the same species" and the mixing of the "bloods" of races always brings about the loss of the superior race's greatness.

These strangely familiar words are more than faint remembrances of Hitler's radio broadcasts. You may have heard these same false ideas across the backyard fence, in church study groups, at the shop during coffee break, or in the offices of some educational, political, business, and labor leaders I know.[2]

One should not lose sight of the fact that Chalk's radio address hit the airwaves in 1968, just over twenty years following the end of World War II. The atrocities of the Nazi regime remained fresh in the minds of Americans, and Chalk's comparison between ordinary US citizens and the ideology of Hitler surely caught their attention.

Later in that same sermon, Chalk suggested that racism caused Christians to misinterpret the Great Commission of Jesus. In a passage often quoted in Churches of Christ sermons and one particularly important to Chalk's Southern Evangelical listeners (Matt. 28:16–20), Jesus commanded his followers to preach the gospel to the entire world. Tragically, however, Chalk said, "Racism would modify Christ's words to mean, 'Go ye therefore and teach your own kind,' or even worse, 'Go ye therefore and teach all nations, making sure to keep them in their place.' I can painfully testify that as Christians duped by racism bowing before that false god instead of Jehovah God, we have set out to evangelize Africa while segregating our own churches of America."[3] Chalk's words once again highlighted the ways in which Americans viewed themselves as the saviors of the world (Europe and Africa especially), but at the same time, they remained blind to their own need for salvation.

---

[2] John Allen Chalk, "Hatred Is Only Skin Deep," in *Three American Revolutions* (Carlton Press, 1970), 71.

[3] Chalk, "Hatred Is Only Skin Deep," 73.

Moving beyond the theoretical and toward the practical, Chalk asked his audience, "What would be your attitude toward the first White on your block who sold his house to a Negro family? Would you stay? Would you sell? What would you vote for if your church decided to leave such a neighborhood?"[4] As the 1960s progressed, more and more White Americans found ways to distance themselves from their Black counterparts. Thousands of White private Christian schools emerged across the South to prevent White and Black children from attending public school together. Likewise, numerous White Christian congregations sold their inner-city church buildings and moved to the suburbs to escape the influx of Black citizens (and potential guests or new members to their congregations). In his addresses, Chalk chastised his predominantly White audience for their hypocrisy.

Throughout the four sermons, Chalk pointedly charged Christians with the sin of racism, casting racism as a moral issue, not simply a political or social issue. He said, "Where racism flourishes Christianity dies," challenging the notion that a White Christian could be both a devout follower of Jesus and exhibit the kind of behavior that alienated Blacks.[5] Rather than White Christians treating Black Christians as their brothers and sisters in Christ and leading in efforts to combat the effect of racism on the nation, he lamented that "Christianity has failed to answer the challenge of racism."[6] In his final sermon, Chalk attempted to place White Christians in the shoes of their Black counterparts by offering a testimony given by a Black member of the denomination:

> Not long ago, a Negro said to me: "If I am rejected because
> I am uneducated, just tell me, and I'll go back to school. If
> you want nothing to do with me because of the way I dress,
> just tell me, and I will try to change that. If you don't like the
> place I live, I could move. But if I am rejected because of my

---

4 Chalk, "Hatred Is Only Skin Deep," 74.

5 Chalk, "Hatred Is Only Skin Deep," 75.

6 Chalk, "Hatred Is Only Skin Deep," 75.

color, then there is nothing I can do about that. That's the
way God made me."[7]

Twenty-first-century listeners may also notice some places where Chalk's sermons could have gone further. For example, Chalk discussed racism only in terms of its effects on individuals, failing to articulate the systemic causes and effects of racism on US society. Likewise, much like other White moderates of his time (including Billy Graham), Chalk suggested that racism would cease if only individuals would change their hearts and follow Jesus. Although he did not acknowledge or address the systemic nature of racism in the United States, Chalk's words did sound a dissonant chord among White members of Churches of Christ in 1968.

In the weeks following the broadcast of "Three American Revolutions," *Herald of Truth* offices received scores of letters from around the globe. According to Chalk, the vast majority of those letters offered support for his position and to *Herald of Truth* for their courage in tackling the issue in such a public and bold way. Approximately five hundred people wrote to *Herald of Truth* about the series, and 350 of those spoke specifically about the sermons centering on race. According to analysis conducted by historian Barclay Key, 80 percent of the listeners offered support for the sermons. Nevertheless, when examined by region, the percentages change considerably. For example, over one hundred letters originated from Tennessee, Arkansas, and Texas. From those Southern states, the approval rate hovered around 73 percent. As one moves into the deeper South (Alabama and Mississippi), the approval rate was less than 50 percent.[8] Regardless of their approval or disapproval of Chalk's messages, however, members of Churches of Christ did respond to the series, thereby breaking the sheer silence of the denomination on the subjects of race and racism.

---

[7] Chalk, "Are You a Respecter of Persons?," in *Three American Revolutions*, 103.

[8] Barclay Key, *Race and Restoration: Churches of Christ and the Black Freedom Struggle* (Louisiana State University Press, 2020), 157.

When questioned about that particular season of his life, Chalk talks mostly about the positive reaction of his listeners, but a perusal of Chalk's personal letters from 1968 (especially those written to him by his friends) indicates a time of severe trial.[9] Walter Burch, for example, wrote multiple letters to Chalk during this period, and each correspondence made attempts to encourage and build up the radio host. Burch sought to help Chalk understand that others stood with him in the fight against denominational prejudice and racism.[10]

Further Evidence of Chalk's Voice

Although Chalk's series on *Herald of Truth* garnered the most attention, other lesser-known events from his life bear witness to his dedication to combat racism with Churches of Christ. Shortly following the death of Martin Luther King Jr., Chalk wrote a letter to Reuel Lemmons, then editor of *Firm Foundation*. In that correspondence, Chalk requested that Lemmons include a tribute to King in *Firm Foundation*. Lemmons's response to Chalk reflects the most common attitude among White denominational leaders of the time. Refusing to publish the tribute, Lemmons questioned King's allegiance to Jesus and referred to him as a modernist, a lawbreaker, and a Communist.[11] Even though Lemmons did not grant Chalk's request, the fact that Chalk solicited such a powerful member of the denomination to include a tribute to the most prominent leader of the civil rights movement exemplified Chalk's dedication to this cause. Modeling even greater courage, following Lemmons's refusal to publish the tribute, Chalk wrote a personal letter to the editor once again and openly expressed his belief that Lemmons's position would encourage the racism existent within Churches of Christ to persist.[12]

---

[9] John Allen Chalk, interview with author, May 1, 2024.

[10] Walter Burch to John Allen Chalk, July 23, 1968, John Allen Chalk Papers, Harding University Special Collections, https://scholarworks.harding.edu/hst-chalk-personal/6261.

[11] Reuel Lemmons to John Allen Chalk, May 16, 1968, John Allen Chalk Papers, box 1968 D–Z Correspondence, Folder L, Harding University Special Collections.

[12] John Allen Chalk to Reuel Lemmons, September 26, 1968, John Allen Chalk Papers, box 1968 D–Z Correspondence, Folder L, Harding University Special Collections.

Chalk also took part in denominational workshops centered on the work of racial reconciliation. He participated in the invitation-only meeting held in Nashville in 1966 that brought together prominent White and Black leaders of Churches of Christ to discuss the problem of racism within the denomination. In 1968, he served as the keynote speaker at a meeting in Dayton, Ohio, and attended two other workshops, one in Nashville and the other in Atlanta. Each of these meetings centered on the topic of racism, and each had as its mission the reorientation of the denomination toward racial equality.

During the 1968 Atlanta workshop, Chalk made the comment that the *Herald of Truth* must be prepared to die, if necessary, in order to transmit God's truth on racial justice.[13] Most workshop attendees signed a statement indicating their commitment to racial equality and their promise to take concrete steps to move Churches of Christ in that direction. Many college administrators refused to sign the statement, and some church leaders, including elders from the Highland Church of Christ in Abilene (which oversaw the *Herald of Truth*), also refused to sign. Chalk, even though his direct supervisors refused to sign, added his name to the document, knowing the statement would be published in a denominational journal shortly after the conclusion of the workshop.

Numerous other moments from Chalk's life reveal his incredible passion for racial equality. Batsell Barrett Baxter, a prominent preacher and writer within Churches of Christ, as well as the most prominent face of the *Herald of Truth* television program for many years, did not appreciate Chalk's series, "Three American Revolutions." In multiple letters written between the two men in 1968, they refer to a tense conversation they had face-to-face. Despite the disapproval of his mentor, Chalk continued to support his decision to openly address racism on the *Herald of Truth*.[14]

---

[13] Walter Burch to John Allen Chalk, July 1, 1968, John Allen Chalk Papers, Harding University Special Collections, https://scholarworks.harding.edu/hstchalk-personal/6275.

[14] John Allen Chalk to Batsell Barrett Baxter, July 15, 1968, John Allen Chalk Papers, Harding University Special Collections, https://scholarworks.harding.edu/hst-chalk-personal/6277.

Carl Cheatham, university minister for a campus ministry to Oklahoma State University in Stillwater, Oklahoma, sent a letter to Chalk in 1968 asking for his recommendations to fill a new ministry position. The search team sought to hire a graduate student to evangelize the campus. Chalk promptly sent a letter recommending Ivory James, a Black minister, for the post. He wrote to Cheatham, "Even though it might come as an initial shock, I believe that there are several advantages in bringing a man like Ivory James to the church there and to the campus of Oklahoma State University."[15] One of the commitments made by attendees at the Atlanta workshop centered on using influence to lobby for racial equality within Churches of Christ. This correspondence between Chalk and Cheatham provides evidence that Chalk took that commitment seriously.

In addition to his own activism, Chalk also supported the efforts of others seeking racial equality. In 1968, Nashville Christian Institute, a school established to educate Black children in Nashville, closed. The predominantly White board of directors took the proceeds from the sale of the property and used them to establish a scholarship for Black students at the recently desegregated David Lipscomb College. Many Black members of the denomination expressed their frustration with the decision, and numerous alumni of Nashville Christian Institute took the board to court. During this episode, R. N. Hogan, a prominent Black leader within Churches of Christ, wrote a stinging article in *The Christian Echo* and referred to the actions of the board as "the grab of the century."[16] Two months after Hogan's article appeared, Chalk sent Hogan a letter to express his support. He referred to Hogan's words as "an honest and loving explanation" of the entire situation.[17]

---

[15] John Allen Chalk to Carl W. Cheatham, July 16, 1968, John Allen Chalk Papers, Harding University Special Collections, https://scholarworks.harding.edu/hstchalk-personal/6275.

[16] Richard N. Hogan, "The Grab of the Century," *Christian Echo* 63, no. 11 (1968): 1. For a detailed narrative of this event, see Wes Crawford, *Shattering the Illusion: How African American Churches of Christ Moved from Segregation to Independence* (Abilene Christian University Press, 2013), 125–41.

[17] John Allen Chalk to Richard N. Hogan, January 10, 1969, John Allen Chalk Papers, Harding University Special Collections, https://scholarworks.harding.edu/hst-chalk-personal/6494.

Following the death of Marshall Keeble, Lemmons published a tribute to the Black evangelist in *Firm Foundation*. The article praised Keeble's humility and attacked the strategies of King and other civil rights leaders. Chalk wrote Lemmons multiple letters about the article, and in those letters, he mentioned his frustration with Lemmons's assertion that an "infinitesimally small amount of racial prejudice" existed within Churches of Christ.[18] Unable to get Lemmons's attention on his own, Chalk solicited the help of Norman Adamson, a Black associate minister at Stony Island Church of Christ in Chicago (a predominantly White congregation). He urged Adamson to reach out to Lemmons with his own perceptions of the article, hoping Lemmons would come to understand the ways in which his article hurt Black members of the denomination. He wrote to Adamson, "I did not want to see this form of implicit racism, or, at the least, ignorance of the true situation, to pass without some effort to speak to it."[19]

Preceding the 1968 Race Conference in Atlanta, Chalk wrote multiple letters to specific members of the denomination to attend. Jimmy Allen, who sent personal letters to invitees on Harding College letterhead, let Chalk know who had not responded to those invitations. Chalk then took it upon himself to follow up with those individuals, urging them to attend the workshop.[20] These examples bear witness to Chalk's habit of publicly and privately aiding in the cause of racial reconciliation, sometimes on his own and often through his encouragement of others.

One important trait among White civil rights leaders often unnoticed or ignored involves education. A White person will never fully understand or appreciate the effects of racism felt by Black Americans. No amount of study or research will grant a White parent the ability to understand the emotions stirring in a Black parent who must explain racism to his or her child for the first time. A White scholar

---

[18] Reuel Lemmons, "Marshall Keeble," *Firm Foundation* 85, no. 20 (1968): 306.

[19] John Allen Chalk to Norman Adamson, May 20, 1968, John Allen Chalk Papers, Harding University Special Collections, https://scholarworks.harding.edu/hst-chalk-personal/6240.

[20] John Allen Chalk to George Bailey, June 17, 1968, John Allen Chalk Papers, Harding University Special Collections, https://scholarworks.harding.edu/hst-chalk-personal/6274.

who studies and writes about slavery, segregation, and ongoing racism in the United States will never fully comprehend the fear a young Black man feels when a police car moves behind his vehicle. Nevertheless, one should notice when White Americans take steps to understand better. In January 1968, Chalk wrote a letter to his friend and ministerial colleague, Zebedee Bishop, that displayed this desire to better understand the perspectives of Black Americans. In that letter, Chalk asked Bishop, a Black minister in Detroit, for permission to call upon him on occasion for his perspective on the race crisis in the world. He wrote, "You can bring a kind of enlightenment to my own study and sensitivity that I could not have otherwise."[21] One wonders how the race crisis in the United States would evolve if White and Black Americans sought to understand one another better.

One final hallmark of Chalk's activism demands attention. It manifested itself clearly in correspondence between Chalk and one of his ministry friends, Charles Shelton, in 1968. Shelton, a leader in the campus evangelism movement within Churches of Christ, wrote a letter to Chalk, urging his friend to be patient with White leaders of the Union Avenue Church of Christ in Memphis, Tennessee, who were slow in their advancement of congregational desegregation. Shelton agreed with Chalk's position but urged him to have patience as the older leaders gradually moved in a new direction. In response, Chalk wrote:

> Charles, your letter reflects a white mentality. I see in your letter no tears, no laments, no heartaches for the black man's plight in America. I see no realistic grappling with the established racist structures in the Church of Christ. Your attitude is the kind that will allow racists to continue to control all our Christian colleges, all our brotherhood papers, all leadership positions in local churches throughout the country. Has not

---

[21] John Allen Chalk to Zebedee Bishop, January 9, 1969, John Allen Chalk Papers, Harding University Special Collections, https://scholarworks.harding.edu/hst-chalk-personal/6280.

the civil rights movement taught us that progress only comes when struggle and tension occur at the sources of power?

When I see Norvel Young unwilling to this date to use the word "black" in public when referring to Negroes, when I see Reuel Lemmons state that there is almost no racial prejudice in churches of Christ, and when I see the white back-lash or, as Humphrey Foutz chooses to call it, "the continuation of white racism," continuing in everything being done by the officials of churches of Christ, I cannot help but think that your letter only aids and abets these evil situations. My reaction, therefore, is to the fact that you have counseled gradualism at a time when America is burning; that your letter has urged me to so understand the Union Avenue leadership that I could under no possible circumstances be able to provide any kind of tension and confrontation of their lives with the absolute claims of Jesus Christ.[22]

Gradualism became a hallmark strategy of White moderates in the 1960s. Although not lobbying against racial equality, many White leaders felt aligned with the cause for civil rights because they advocated for eventual change. In King's most famous writing, the "Letter from Birmingham Jail," he addressed his words to eight White clergymen from Birmingham. Most of these men would be counted among the White moderates who urged the US public to embrace racial equality, but not yet. In any era, White moderates consider themselves enlightened and allies of more persistent protesters, but King reminded those eight Alabama clergymen (and the millions of others who read his letter) that gradualism does not work. During a poignant moment in his letter, King discussed the immorality of waiting for justice, introducing this topic with the now famous words: "justice too long delayed is

---

[22] John Chalk to Charles Shelton, March 19, 1969, John Allen Chalk Papers, box 1969 Correspondence, Harding University Special Collections.

justice denied."[23] A few months later, while standing on the steps of the Lincoln Memorial in Washington, DC, King referred to gradualism as a "tranquilizing drug."[24] Chalk's words to Shelton indicate his agreement with King on this issue.

Because he challenged the racist status quo of Churches of Christ publicly and privately in the late 1960s, Chalk received more than his fair share of criticism. To catch a glimpse of the ire many within Churches of Christ aimed at Chalk, one could read an article published by Noble Patterson in his *Christian Journal* (another denominational periodical). Shortly after King's death, Patterson used his platform to castigate King for his activism and theology, and Patterson also criticized "one of our young and dynamic radio evangelists" who had recently praised King in a sermon. Without Patterson calling Chalk by name, most readers of his journal understood his clear reference. Following Chalk's decision to sign the statement at the Atlanta race relations workshop, letters poured into the *Herald of Truth* offices (many from donors to the ministry), demanding an explanation.[25] By the end of 1969, they received at least one letter every week from one of the two thousand congregations that financially supported the ministry. Years later, Chalk would describe that season simply as a "tough time."[26]

Considering how dissonant Chalk's voice sounded next to the dominant sounds coming from other Church of Christ leaders in the late 1960s, one should not be surprised to learn that he exited ministry in the early 1970s. Following Chalk's brief tenure at the *Herald of Truth* (from 1966 to 1969), he spent an even briefer season as the pulpit minister at Highland Church of Christ. He preached his last sermon on the last Sunday in May 1971. The very next morning, he began law school at The University of Texas at Austin. Even before he left his post at Highland, Chalk wrote to a good friend, Walter Burch, "I find it very

---

[23] Martin Luther King Jr., "Letter from Birmingham Jail," in *The Autobiography of Martin Luther King, Jr.*, ed. Clayborne Carson (Warner Books, 1998), 192.

[24] King, "I Have a Dream," in *The Autobiography of Martin Luther King, Jr.*, 224.

[25] Key, *Race and Restoration*, 155.

[26] Chalk, "Turbulent Years."

difficult not to begin seriously looking for some other role in which I can make a meaningful contribution as a Christian, but not be on the 'dole' of the institutional church."[27] Less than two years after Chalk wrote these words, he was actively seeking new ways to make his contribution.

For over fifty years, Chalk has practiced law, most of those years as an attorney in Fort Worth. In that span, he has earned too many awards and accolades to mention, garnering a reputation as a fair and compassionate litigator who relates well to his clients.[28] One could argue that Chalk has continued his work for social justice in the courtroom. Although unable to push an entire denomination toward racial equality, Chalk has used the courtroom to seek and find justice for countless families over the past half-century. When given the opportunity to reflect on his life as a minister and a lawyer, he says he was happy in his first career as a church minister and radio evangelist, but then he got a higher calling—the law.[29]

---

[27] John Allen Chalk to Walter Burch, November 12, 1969, John Allen Chalk Papers, box 1969 Correspondence, Harding University Special Collections.

[28] "Reflections on a Radio Minister Turned Employment Lawyer," *Texas Super Lawyers* (Sep. 14, 2007).

[29] "Reflections on a Radio Minister Turned Employment Lawyer."

The Chorus

If one ventured into the church buildings and onto the campuses associated with Churches of Christ in the mid-twentieth century, and if one happened to pick up and read a copy of the *Gospel Advocate*, *Firm Foundation*, or most other periodicals associated with this predominantly Southern Christian denomination, one would hear mostly silence regarding the racial revolution raging through the streets of the United States. Nevertheless, a few bold and courageous White leaders broke the silence. In addition to Carl Spain, John Allen Chalk, and Walter Burch, several other White leaders joined their voices to create a small chorus, crying out against the racial status quo. This final chapter will allow leaders to lean in closely to hear the melody of their song.

Dwain Evans (1933–)

Dwain Evans was born near Palmer, Texas, on April 4, 1933. As a child of the Great Depression, he spent his earliest years in dire poverty, moving from farming community to farming community across the dust bowl as his father, who suffered from paranoid schizophrenia, tried to eke out a living for his growing family. Until he reached high school, his various homes came equipped only with an outhouse. Local congregations of the Churches of Christ often provided food and shelter for Evans's family, which certainly endeared him to the church and instilled within him a passion to help the less-fortunate members of society.[1] Evans recalls that one of his daily responsibilities in his grade school years involved walking the family's Jersey cow to different vacant lots each morning so the cow could graze.[2] He feared the contempt of his classmates should they ever catch a glimpse of his daily chore.

In addition to the hurdles caused by poverty, Evans also had to scale the obstacles in front of him related to his physical body. Born with a clubfoot, he endured numerous surgeries throughout his life to help him walk correctly and without pain. As one might expect, his peers ridiculed him and his condition mercilessly, which included giving him the unique nickname: "flat-foot floogie with a floy, floy."[3]

Without question, however, the greatest challenge during Evans's childhood occurred during his junior high years. Before his family truly understood the severity of his father's condition, his paranoid schizophrenia led to tragedy. Evans's father came home early one afternoon from work, sat down his lunch box on the counter, and then, without warning, pulled out his pistol and shot his son-in-law in the back five times, killing him almost instantly. Shortly after this incident, his father received his diagnosis and was remanded to the State Hospital in Terrell, Texas, to be confined in the unit for the criminally insane.[4]

Each of these life experiences provides context for the ways in which Evans routinely identified with the less fortunate or with those who had to overcome incredible obstacles. Although many White leaders

---

[1] For insight into Evans's early life, see Dwain Evans, "Evans: A Memoir," in *Restoring the* First-Century *Church in the* Twenty-First *Century: Essays on the Stone–Campbell Restoration Movement*, ed. Warren Lewis and Hans Rollman (Wipf and Stock, 2005), 443–60.

[2] Evans, "Evans: A Memoir," 444.

[3] Evans, "Evans: A Memoir," 443.

[4] Evans, "Evans: A Memoir," 447–48.

in Churches of Christ remained deaf to the cries of Black Americans, Evans heard their voices, and he added his own voice to the small chorus of people demanding change.

Evans became visible within Churches of Christ because of his leadership in what became known as the Exodus Movement.[5] After attending Abilene Christian College in the early 1950s and graduating with a degree in Bible and ministry, he preached at several small congregations throughout Texas and even spent three years in Augusta, Maine, ministering at a small congregation sponsored by the Skillman Avenue Church of Christ in Dallas. While in Maine, he developed a passion for church planting, and he determined to gather at least ten families to join him in planting a new Christian community in the "unchurched" Northeast United States. He and his family moved back to Texas to finish his education, gather financial support, and form a team of families to join them. On the first Sunday of August 1963, the Evans family and over eighty other families began worshiping on Long Island at a congregation that would become the West Islip Church of Christ.[6] This incredible feat even caught the attention of the national press. *Time* magazine ran a story titled "The Campbellites Are Coming" on February 15, 1963, and the story also appeared in the *Fort Worth Star-Telegram, Newsday* (Long Island), and many other national papers.[7] This incredible accomplishment also earned Evans a place at the table among other Church of Christ leaders.

A well-known and respected preacher and church planter within the denomination, Evans used his positional power and influence to challenge the racial status quo. By 1966, the Exodus Movement had received national attention, and Evans had become a well-known preacher within the denomination; his speaking calendar included engagements all over the United States. In that year, his alma mater, Abilene Christian College, invited him to deliver an address titled "Exodus and the Bible."

---

[5] P. Kent Smith, "Exodus Movement of the 1960s," in *The Encyclopedia of the Stone-Campbell Movement*, ed. Douglas A. Foster et al. (Eerdmans, 2005), 324–25.

[6] Evans, "Evans: A Memoir," 455.

[7] Evans, "Evans: A Memoir," 454.

During his sermon, Evans made the case that the Holy Spirit influenced the lives of Christians apart from the word of Scripture. Most members of the denomination held a "Word only" view of the Holy Spirit in the mid-twentieth century, so Evans's words struck a dissonant chord with many in the audience.[8] In those days, speakers regularly delivered the same address on two different days. Following the first address, three members of the university administration pulled him aside and encouraged him strongly to deliver a different sermon the following night. One of them even remarked in that conversation, "Dwain, it is a shame for you to throw away your career over a little thing like this."[9] Compelled by his belief that his conclusions were just and correct, however, Evans proceeded as planned and delivered that same address the next day.

The fallout came swiftly. Before the lectureship, Evans had speaking engagements across the United States booked regularly through 1975 (nine years later). Following the event in Abilene, all but two of those invitations were rescinded. He also lost his regular column in *The Christian Chronicle*, a notable periodical associated with the denomination. Future invitations to speak on the campuses of Abilene Christian College, David Lipscomb College, and Oklahoma Christian College were all rescinded. After 1966, only Pepperdine allowed Evans on campus to speak. Closer to home, the West Islip membership began to dip. Before the lecture, attendance had grown to over four hundred people each week; following the address, the congregation shrunk to half that size.[10] Although the 1966 lectureship sermon did not center on race, racism, or segregation, this episode does shine a light on Evans's courage to speak boldly about controversial issues. He did not shy away from controversy, and he (like so many others) paid a hefty price.

This same courageous spirit emboldened his speech about race. Even before Evans earned respectability within Churches of Christ, he

---

[8] For a discussion of this view of the Holy Spirit and the controversy it produced within Churches of Christ, see Richard Hughes and James T. Gorman, *Reviving the Ancient Faith: The Story of Churches of Christ in America*, 3rd ed. (Eerdmans, 2024), 69–70, 255–56.

[9] Evans, "Evans: A Memoir," 458.

[10] Evans, "Evans: A Memoir," 458.

showed signs of standing with Black Americans. In 1954, not long after the *Brown v. Board of Education* decision, while serving as a minister in Coolidge, Texas, Evans tackled the topic of segregation. Working at his first congregation at only twenty-one years of age, Evans wrote a bulletin article on the second chapter of James. In his rendering of the text, he inserted the word "black man" instead of "poor man," and he used "white man" instead of "rich man."[11] This decision led to a serious confrontation with one member of his congregation, but Evans, although young and inexperienced, refused to back down and let it be known that he would follow the Bible on these matters. A few years later, in 1960, while preaching for the Parkway Drive Church of Christ in Lubbock, Texas, Evans preached a sermon titled "Is Segregation Scriptural?" Even though members threatened to leave the congregation and pull their support, Evans continued to move his congregation toward integration.[12]

The most noteworthy example of Evans's activism centers on the 1968 race relations workshop in Atlanta (discussed in Chapter Five). Evans worked closely (and behind the scenes) with Walter Burch to organize, plan, and orchestrate that important event. Because he and Burch had already estranged themselves from so many White power brokers of the denomination by 1968, they pushed Jimmy Allen, Roosevelt Wells, and Eugene Lawton to the forefront of this effort to add credibility and increase participation in the meeting. Nevertheless, those involved with the event credited Burch and Evans for leading the effort. This workshop brought together key White and Black leaders of Churches of Christ to deliver and hear presentations on racism within the denomination. At the conclusion of that event, most attendees signed a "Statement of Acknowledgement of Racial Prejudice and Proposals for Improving

---

[11] Evans, "Evans: A Memoir," 451. See also Freda Elliott Baker, "Exodus/Bay Shore: How an Idea Became a Reality," West Islip (New York) Church of Christ Audio Collection, Center for Restoration Studies, Abilene Christian University, https://digitalcommons.acu.edu/west_islip/13.

[12] Evans, "Evans: A Memoir," 452–53.

Race Relations in Churches of Christ," a manifesto that later appeared in a full-page display in *The Christian Chronicle*.[13]

During that same summer, Burch, Evans, and others worked to create a special issue of *20th Century Christian* in July of 1968. That special issue, titled "Christ and Race Relations," included articles from thirteen White authors and five Black authors, most of them well-situated in positions of leadership within Churches of Christ, including Bill Banowsky (associate editor of the journal and newly appointed president of Pepperdine College); John Allen Chalk (preacher at Highland Church of Christ in Abilene, Texas, and primary voice for the *Herald of Truth* radio show); Ira North (preacher at Madison Church of Christ in Madison, Tennessee); Walter Burch (public relations consultant and church leader); and Carl Spain (professor of Bible at Abilene Christian College).

Evans offered his own contribution to the *20th Century Christian* publication, titled "Jesus Speaks on Race Relations." His article opens with these pointed questions:

> "So whatever you wish that men would do to you, do also to them: for this is the law and the prophets." Do you remember the separate water fountains in the department store? One was marked for white people and the other for colored people. From which do you suppose Jesus would have drunk? Or how about the restroom behind the service station? Have you forgotten about that?[14]

Throughout his article, he routinely compared the words of Jesus with the customs of the US South. He boldly challenged his readers to put the confrontational ethics of Jesus into practice.

The pressures of ministry became too much for Evans's family. Barbara Evans, Dwain's wife, never fully embraced the idea of becoming

---

[13] See "Atlanta Race Relations Conference Lists Recommendations for Improvement," *Christian Chronicle* 25, no. 40 (1968): 4.

[14] Dwain Evans, "Jesus Speaks on Race Relations," *20th Century Christian* 30, no. 10 (1968): 22.

a minister's wife, and in 1970, four grueling years following the 1966 Abilene Christian College Lectureship, she informed her husband about her intense dissatisfaction. Following a time of marital counseling, the couple decided to exit the West Islip Church of Christ and chart a new path for their lives together. Those who added their voices to the chorus crying out against racial injustice paid the price. Many of them lost their jobs, quite a few of them were threatened with violence or death, and virtually all of them exited ministry by the end of the 1960s. Evans's name finds its way onto that long list of persecuted prophets, but there are others.

Lawrence "Bud" Stumbaugh (1940–)

Lawrence "Bud" Stumbaugh entered this world in 1940 in Pensacola, Florida. After only one year, his father abandoned the family, and Stumbaugh's mother moved with her four children to Selma, Alabama, to be closer to her parents. He considered the infamous civil rights town home until he graduated from David Lipscomb College in 1962. Not only did he live most of his early years in the town infamous for Bloody Sunday, but he also ministered at Homewood Church of Christ in Birmingham, Alabama, the site of one of King's most famous campaigns, in the mid-1960s. He also preached for congregations in New York City and Jonesboro, Arkansas. Stumbaugh's entire ministerial career, however, lasted only a few years (from 1962 until 1967), because he refused to remain silent.

Not long after he graduated from David Lipscomb College, Stumbaugh met with Athens Clay Pullias, then president of the institution. During the meeting, Pullias requested a financial donation to the school from one of the newly minted alumni of the college, but Stumbaugh refused. The young, inexperienced minister told the powerful president, "I will never give money to this institution as long as it is segregated." With those words, Pullias (a well-known segregationist) accused Stumbaugh of being a radical and threw him out of his office.[15]

---

[15] Lawrence Stumbaugh, interview with author, December 8, 2023.

After preaching from 1962 until 1965 for the Queens Church of Christ in New York City, he moved to the Deep South. His tenure at the Homewood Church of Christ in Birmingham lasted only one year, however, because the young preacher delivered a sermon on God's desire for integration. Just two years following King's famous visit to "Bombingham" (a nickname given to the city in the 1960s because of the number of brick homes and church buildings bombed during that period), Stumbaugh preached about the immorality of segregation from one of its pulpits. In the days and weeks following that sermon, Stumbaugh received death threats on his home phone, and he recalls being afraid to start his car every morning, fearing someone may have placed a bomb in it overnight.[16]

Between the time he preached that sermon and when he was fired for preaching that sermon, Stumbaugh returned home to visit his family in Selma. While there, he accepted an invitation to preach at one of the local Church of Christ congregations. Once again exemplifying his undaunted courage, he spoke on the topic of race. When he arrived back home in Birmingham, his answering machine contained numerous threats, including some threats to take his life. One person said, "If you ever come back to Selma and preach a message like that again, you'll never make it out of town alive." The elders of the Homewood congregation fired Stumbaugh from his post, and numerous speaking invitations to other congregations were rescinded.[17]

When he left Birmingham, Stumbaugh looked for a congregation that would accept his views on race and segregation. To measure his theological fit with other congregations, he preached his sermon on race and integration each time he tried out for a new preaching post. He attempted desperately to find a church home that would embrace him, his views, and his family. Finally, he landed at the Frierson Street Church of Christ in Jonesboro, Arkansas, in 1966. Although the Frierson Street congregation may have been comfortable with his

---

¹⁶ Stumbaugh, interview with author.
¹⁷ Stumbaugh, interview with author.

countercultural positions, other Christians in the area quickly revolted. Part of his duties with the congregation involved preaching weekly on a regional radio broadcast, and during one of those sermons, Stumbaugh expressed his frustration with people denying Black Americans the right to seek an education at colleges and universities that at the time catered only to White students. During his remarks, he mentioned the courage of James Meredith, who broke the color line at the University of Mississippi in 1962. Not long after that broadcast, a group of White preachers from area Churches of Christ met with Stumbaugh to express their disdain for his message. One preacher revealed that, as a fellow preacher in the Churches of Christ, he was ashamed of Stumbaugh's position on integration.[18] Undeterred, Stumbaugh presented a similar address at the 1966 Alabama Christian College Lectureship.[19]

Mirroring the series of events that transpired in Birmingham, Stumbaugh once again received threats to his life, and during that season, he began to rethink his call to ministry. Recalling that season of his life, he said he had to determine whether he could continue to draw a paycheck from the church and speak the truth at the same time. He worried about the financial future and physical safety of his wife and children, but he could not preach without speaking about race, racism, and integration. Weighing all his options, he made the decision to leave congregational ministry in 1967. He went on to achieve incredible success in the insurance business (founding and leading a multimillion-dollar company). He served on numerous nonprofit boards, authored a book, became a sought-after motivational speaker, was awarded an honorary doctorate from Faulkner University, and even served eight terms as a Georgia state senator. In these roles and with these credentials, Stumbaugh sought equality for all persons, but regrettably, he concluded the pulpit provided too great an obstacle for that brand of justice.

---

[18] Stumbaugh, interview with author.

[19] John Allen Chalk to Lawrence Stumbaugh, June 28, 1966, John Allen Chalk Collection, John Allen Chalk: Personal Correspondence, Harding University Special Collections.

Stumbaugh's most poignant moment as a civil rights activist and as a Church of Christ leader came in 1968 during the race relations workshop in Nashville. In addition to working with David Jones, preaching minister for the Schrader Lane Church of Christ, to organize the event, Stumbaugh also delivered the hardest-hitting sermon of the workshop. When compared to Spain's 1960 Abilene Christian College Lectureship speech, "Modern Challenges to Christian Morals," which continues to reverberate across the denomination today, Stumbaugh's address received hardly any attention at all. The Nashville meeting was not well-attended (especially by White members of the denomination), and none of the race relations workshops (in 1966 or 1968) compared in size to the crowds of the lectureships that took place on college campuses. The fact that so few people heard or later read Stumbaugh's address, which appeared in the special edition of *The Christian Chronicle* in May 1968, stands as a great tragedy. No other address delivered or article written on this topic in the history of Churches of Christ more clearly and comprehensively attacked the principles and justifications bolstering slavery, racism, and segregation. As a trained rhetorician (and skilled politician), Stumbaugh went point by point, debunking every significant argument raised by Whites to justify their racist practices and responded thoughtfully and theologically to those who habitually and uncritically denounced civil rights activists. (That entire address may be found in Appendix F in the back of this book.)

Toward the beginning of his sermon, Stumbaugh challenged the major tenets of scientific racism. By the eighteenth and nineteenth centuries, Western scientists joined other supporters of slavery in finding ways to justify the peculiar institution. Among them, Harvard professor Nathan Southgate Shaler began articulating his theory of retrogression, the dangerous notion that Black-skinned people, left unattended by their White masters, would regress to their natural state of savagery.[20] Like Spain did in his 1960 lectureship address, Stumbaugh compared these notions to the racial ideology that motivated the Nazis in Germany,

---

[20] Nathaniel Southgate Shaler, "The Negro Problem," *Atlantic Monthly* 54 (Nov. 1884): 42.

but he said, "the Nazi genocide of this century seems almost like a game of hide-and-seek" compared to the sixty million Africans transported on slave ships against their will across the Atlantic Ocean.[21] He told his audience, "Why those of us who are the descendants of the slave runners and slave owners of yesteryear should be shocked at Hitler's theory of the master race, and his consequent debasement and cruel treatment of those he termed inferior, is one of the inconsistencies of our reasoning processes I will never understand." To those who would rebut his logic, pointing out the widespread poverty and presumed intellectual deficiencies of Black Americans in the mid-twentieth century as proof of their innate inferiority, Stumbaugh offered compelling reasons for the then current state of the Black community in the United States. Succinctly stated, Whites had denied Blacks access to education and financial security. Worse yet, "the very people who had amputated his legs were now criticizing the black man for being a cripple."[22]

Supporters of slavery in the United States justified their positions not only with science, but also with Scripture, and Stumbaugh next took aim at those inept biblical scholars. "White supremacy," he said, "was literally defended with the Bible in hand."[23] After calling attention to the ways in which preachers and church leaders twisted Scripture to justify their support of slavery, Stumbaugh offered passages that admonished people of faith to show no partiality (James 2:1) and to look out for the interests of others over their own (Phil. 2:3).

White Christian supporters of slavery also justified their position by suggesting slavery benefited slaves. According to this logic, White Christians rescued Black Africans from savagery, gifting them with education, civility, and Jesus. One can almost hear the sarcasm dripping from his lips as Stumbaugh said to the crowd in Nashville, "It is strange, indeed, how ungrateful many of these blacks were, for they staged mutinies, leaped into the sea to drown while still chained together, and tried

---

[21] Lawrence Stumbaugh, "Address by Lawrence L. (Bud) Stumbaugh," supplement to *Christian Chronicle* (May 10, 1968): 5.

[22] Stumbaugh, "Address by Lawrence L. (Bud) Stumbaugh," 6.

[23] Stumbaugh, "Address by Lawrence L. (Bud) Stumbaugh," 6.

every known method of suicide to keep from accepting the 'blessing' of living in this 'Christian' nation."[24]

Following his critique of eighteenth- and nineteenth-century slave-holding Christians, Stumbaugh turned his attention to the church of the twentieth century. He called attention to the hypocrisy of preaching about the love of Jesus while refusing to invite Black children to the annual Vacation Bible School. He pointed out the practice of some White congregations to intentionally skip certain streets of their town in evangelistic door-knocking campaigns for fear that those residents might actually show up at church on Sunday. He also criticized the White church for relocating to the suburbs to escape a "predominantly Negro neighborhood" and then patting themselves on the back for selling their old building to the "colored brethren" to pay their new debts. Stumbaugh named this practice "moral bankruptcy" and indicated these examples of degeneracy made him want to throw up.[25] Stumbaugh, reflecting on the current state of the church, finally offered this appraisal: "We have been found deficient in love on the one hand and courage on the other."[26]

Instead of leading the charge toward social equality, the church, according to Stumbaugh, had allowed the schools, the courts, and politicians to chart the path. By allowing those institutions to lead in civil rights activism, the church found license to place segregation under the broad umbrella of "social issues." Countless preachers, editors, and college administrators in Churches of Christ refused to participate in marches or support boycotts or preach against the immorality of racism because, according to them, such activism belonged in the halls of Washington, not the church building. By labeling segregation and racism social or political issues (instead of moral issues), the church abandoned its responsibility to engage and sharply criticized those congregations and clergy who did participate in civil rights

---

24 Stumbaugh, "Address by Lawrence L. (Bud) Stumbaugh," 5.

25 Stumbaugh, "Address by Lawrence L. (Bud) Stumbaugh," 6–7.

26 Stumbaugh, "Address by Lawrence L. (Bud) Stumbaugh," 7.

activism. Stumbaugh lamented that, as equality slowly emerged for Black Americans, citizens of the nation would be forced to say, "Thank the Supreme Court" instead of "Thank God."[27]

To those who really did believe these issues belonged in the courts and not the church, Stumbaugh shined a spotlight on their hypocrisy. He reminded his listeners of the extensive involvement of many Church of Christ congregations in the 1960 presidential campaign. To keep a Catholic out of the White House, many preachers railed against John F. Kennedy from their pulpits, and many congregations passed out tracts in their communities about the dangers of allowing a Catholic to occupy the highest office in the land. He specifically mentioned "pulpit preachments, bulletin articles, special announcements, radio and television programs, and bulk mail-outs on church letterhead" used to denounce Kennedy and his candidacy. In addition to the Kennedy campaign, Stumbaugh mentioned the involvement of Christians in lobbying against the liquor-by-drink referendum in Nashville.[28] Members of the church felt no reservations in blatantly involving themselves in such political matters, but they considered themselves completely justified in vacating any responsibility to engage the most pressing social issue facing the United States in the mid-twentieth century.

Perhaps the most often rehearsed rationale for refusing to engage civil rights activism by Christians in the 1950s and 1960s (or any other decade) centered on the law. Instead of joining civil rights leaders in their campaigns for justice, countless White Christians ridiculed protesters for their lawbreaking tendencies. Stumbaugh spent a great deal of time in his sermon poking holes in this logic. If obeying the law really was of utmost importance to Christians, Stumbaugh wondered why Christians "did not give out tracts on street corners in 1954 supporting not just the need for compliance with the law, but also pointing out that the higher law of love made it imperative that we do the right thing

---

[27] Stumbaugh, "Address by Lawrence L. (Bud) Stumbaugh," 7.
[28] Stumbaugh, "Address by Lawrence L. (Bud) Stumbaugh," 7–8.

for which the Supreme Court justices were calling."[29] If following the law really motivated Christians, why did they celebrate the words of Alabama governor George Wallace, who stubbornly stated his refusal to obey the law during his inaugural address on January 14, 1963, saying, "I say segregation today, segregation tomorrow, segregation forever"?[30]

Stumbaugh also wondered aloud why twentieth-century Christians applauded the patriots at the Boston Tea Party for engaging in civil disobedience against British merchants and the American soldiers who took up arms against leaders of their own country during the Revolutionary War. He noted the gratitude many Americans felt toward those women who lobbied, marched, and protested in favor of women's suffrage.[31] History books contain limitless examples of heroes who lobbied, protested, or fought for their freedom, and most Americans celebrate their heroic feats; nevertheless, when King and other civil rights activists protested in favor of rights for Black Americans, the White church criticized their methods and dismissed them as agitators, lawbreakers, and criminals.

Many White Christians argue that morality cannot be legislated. Stumbaugh retorted, "Of course, it's [sic] true morals cannot be legislated. But behavior can be regulated, and that is what society is trying to do when it passes laws against speeding, bank robbery, murder, and racial discrimination."[32] No law can change a person's heart, but laws do have the power to change behavior, and over time, those changed behaviors can alter the trajectory of a society. Stumbaugh used the analogy of disciplining his children to make his point. The immediate act of discipline does not change his daughter's heart, but it does alter her behavior. He continued, "Many things my daughter does now because I spank her if she does not, she will later do because she sees it is right

---

[29] Stumbaugh, "Address by Lawrence L. (Bud) Stumbaugh," 8.

[30] George Wallace, "The Inaugural Address of Governor George C. Wallace," January 14, 1963, Alabama Department of Archives and History, transcript, https://digital.archives.alabama.gov/digital/collection / voices/id/2952/.

[31] Stumbaugh, "Address by Lawrence L. (Bud) Stumbaugh," 8.

[32] Stumbaugh, "Address by Lawrence L. (Bud) Stumbaugh," 9.

and even enjoyable."[33] In perhaps one of the pointed moments in his sermon, Stumbaugh solidified this point by saying, "Laws can make you quit lynching me, and after all, when you have a rope around my neck, I do not really care if you remove that rope because of love or law, favor or fear, just so long as you remove that rope. I favor more and better legislation in the area of human rights, because I know it can make us treat one another better."[34]

Closely akin to the criticism of civil rights activists for their presumed tendency to break the law was their supposed potential to incite violence, and Stumbaugh addressed this matter with characteristic boldness. The United States had developed a long pattern of violence against Native Americans and against enemies in war, such as the Japanese and Vietnamese. He asked rhetorically, "Haven't we always tried to justify our 'White' violence?"[35] Yet, for some reason, when Black people instigate violence in search for freedom, White people (including White Christians) criticize their methods without paying any attention to their message. Citing examples from history as well as Scripture, Stumbaugh finally concluded that "privileged powers that oppress do not willingly give up their position of dominance. Evil individuals and governments have always had to be pressured into doing right."[36] While discussing violence and power, he articulated his support for the Black Power movement, but he also expressed his hope that Black people would use their power more humanely and morally than White people "in whose hands power has resided for so long."[37]

Toward the conclusion of his address, Stumbaugh sought to measure the effectiveness of the civil rights movement. Too many White Christians criticized the methods of activists and suggested Black people should remain patient for the change that would surely come if more and more people would follow Jesus. Much like Billy Graham

---

[33] Stumbaugh, "Address by Lawrence L. (Bud) Stumbaugh," 9.
[34] Stumbaugh, "Address by Lawrence L. (Bud) Stumbaugh," 8.
[35] Stumbaugh, "Address by Lawrence L. (Bud) Stumbaugh," 9.
[36] Stumbaugh, "Address by Lawrence L. (Bud) Stumbaugh," 9.
[37] Stumbaugh, "Address by Lawrence L. (Bud) Stumbaugh," 10.

and other White moderates in the United States, some White members of Churches of Christ argued that evangelism provided the surest path toward racial equality. Responding to the calls for gradualism and to those who suggested the civil rights movement remained ineffective in its efforts to alter the course of society, Stumbaugh offered a long list of victories for civil rights activists. Just twelve months following the beginning of the sit-in movement in 1960, lunch counters across the South were desegregated. The 1955–56 bus boycott in Montgomery led to the end of segregation on all buses throughout the South. The 1963 Southern Christian Leadership Conference campaign in Birmingham resulted in the Civil Rights Act of 1964, and Bloody Sunday in Selma provided the impetus for the Voting Rights Act of 1965. Stumbaugh concluded that none of these historic changes would have occurred without pressure, and just because some of these events created tension and violence, no one had the right to criticize Black people for this tension and violence. He pointedly told his audience, "To blame those who pressure the white bigots for justice for the hateful reactions of those bigots, is like blaming a doctor for a cancer found upon making exploratory surgery upon his patient."[38]

Stumbaugh's historic address ended with fifteen suggestions to improve race relations, including one that urged people to withdraw from congregations that refused to act according to Christ in these matters. His sermon not only amounted to eloquent rhetoric; he called people to action. The record of Stumbaugh's life (before and after this speech) bears witness to the ways in which he followed his own advice.

Stumbaugh's name can be added to the list that includes Spain, Burch, Chalk, and Evans—White leaders in Churches of Christ who refused to remain silent as Black Christians endured injustice inside and outside the church. But these men were not alone. Prentice Meador Jr., a longtime influential preacher in Churches of Christ, wrote an article titled "20th Century Cargo" for the July 1968 special issue of *20th*

---

[38] Stumbaugh, "Address by Lawrence L. (Bud) Stumbaugh," 10.

Century Christian that discussed the weight of racism on the church.[39] In that same issue, Ira North, longtime preacher at the Madison Church of Christ in Tennessee (at one time the largest Church of Christ congregation in the world), wrote an article in which he encouraged the church to move toward integration.[40] Norvel Young and Bill Banowsky, two influential preachers and college administrators in Churches of Christ, served as editors of *20th Century Christian* and worked with Burch toward the publication of the special issue. Unlike many of his White contemporaries, Banowsky referred to racism as a "spiritual" issue (rather than merely political or social).[41] Billie Sol Estes, a wealthy White member of the denomination, attempted to integrate Abilene Christian College and David Lipscomb College in the early 1960s (unsuccessfully). He personally took Floyd Rose, a young Black member of the denomination, to enroll in Abilene Christian College. When Rose was denied admission, Estes took him across town to McMurry College (a Methodist institution), enrolled him, and paid his tuition.[42] Without question, there are others who, without fanfare or recognition, challenged the racist status quo of Churches of Christ in the twentieth century.

Make no mistake, however, in believing their voices were heard above the silence. The vast majority of White leaders and power brokers of the denomination remained deaf or silent, including the editors of every major denominational journal and the administrators of the denominational colleges. Even Young and Banowsky, who helped produce the special edition of the *20th Century Christian*, showed their consistent apprehension throughout the process of its publication. Certainly, they are to be commended for their courage in publishing this important critique of racism within twentieth-century Churches of Christ; nevertheless, they also barred several articles from the special issue, fearing they would speak too boldly against the racist status quo

---

[39] Prentice A. Meador Jr., "20th Century Cargo," *20th Century Christian* 30, no. 10 (1968): 43–45.

[40] Ira North, "An Integrated Church," *20th Century Christian* 30, no. 10 (1968): 24–25.

[41] William S. Banowsky, "In Him I Say," *20th Century Christian* 30, no. 10 (1968): 2.

[42] Burch, "Race Relations Unpublished Correspondence with Bob Douglas."

of the denomination. As Stumbaugh rightly observed, "If historians a thousand years from now were unable to read any documents other than pamphlets, papers, and magazines written by members of the Church of Christ, they would not be able to discern that America even had a racial problem in the middle years of the twentieth century."[43] For this reason, especially, Churches of Christ remain indebted to the few and courageous members of the chorus who sang into that cavernous hall of prejudice and racism the tunes of equality and justice.

---

[43] Stumbaugh, "Address by Lawrence L. (Bud) Stumbaugh," 8.

Conclusion

Every year on January 15, history repeats itself. Memes begin appearing on Facebook and Instagram pages depicting a familiar quotation of Martin Luther King Jr., often superimposed on top of a picture of King with arms spread wide and voice raised as he delivered his legendary speech from the steps of the Lincoln Memorial. Surprisingly, many of these memes appear on pages managed by White people. White Americans have certainly changed their opinion of King since his assassination over a half-century ago. In the 1960s, most White Americans, including White Christian Americans, dubbed King a lawbreaker, an atheist, an outsider, and a Communist. In the opening decades of the twenty-first century, however, White Americans join Black Americans in celebrating his life and legacy on the holiday created in his honor. Why? What happened in the last half-century to change the minds of so many White Americans?

Certainly, US culture has shifted in significant ways since the 1960s. In the decades following *Brown v. Board of Education*, public schools across the nation finally desegregated. Separate bathrooms, water fountains, and lunch counters no longer exist. Black politicians run for and are elected to office, even the highest office in the land. Thanks to legislation passed in the mid-1960s, Black Americans vote and attend colleges and universities that historically forbade Black students. Two generations of White Americans have grown up with Black Americans in adjacent desks inside the same school buildings and classrooms. For over fifty years, Black and White Americans have eaten together, studied together, attended sporting events together, performed together, and led businesses and created policy together, and a fewer number have even worshiped together. Many White Americans celebrate, along with their Black counterparts, these changes instigated by King and his fellow activists.

In our altered culture, some White Americans make bold claims, such as, "If I had lived in the 1960s, I would have protested with King! I would have participated in the sit-ins, and I would have marched with Black Americans for equality." If White women and men indeed care that much about racial equality, and if they really feel such a strong bond with those who marched, protested, and agitated for civil rights in the middle decades of the twentieth century, they are in luck. Although US culture has shifted in significant ways, racial equality remains unrealized in the opening decades of the twenty-first century, and numerous opportunities exist for White Americans to join their voices today with the chorus of prophets for racial equality from yesterday.

According to the United States Treasury Department, 18.8 percent of Black Americans live in poverty, while only 7.3 percent of White Americans live in poverty. The discrepancy between the household net worth of Black Americans and White Americans has increased significantly since 1989. In 1989, a difference of roughly three hundred thousand dollars existed between Black and White American households; today, that disparity is well over eight hundred thousand dollars. The median household income for Black households in 2020 was $45,870, but for White families, that amount was $74,912.[1]

---

[1] Janis Bowdler and Benjamin Harris, "Racial Inequality in the United States," US Department of the Treasury, July 21, 2022, https://home.treasury.gov/news/featured-stories/racial-inequality-in-the-united-states.

The same disparity exists in the field of education. In 2023, the average SAT score for White American students was 1082 (out of 1600), but for Black American students, that number was only 908.[2] During the 2015–16 school year, Black students made up approximately 15 percent of the United States student population; yet, they made up 35 percent of students who had been suspended once, 44 percent of students who had been suspended more than once, and 36 percent of students who had been expelled.[3]

The disparity between Black and White Americans also appears in health care. Black women are three to four times more likely to experience a pregnancy-related death than White women.[4] The National Library of Medicine and the Centers for Disease Control and Prevention report that "Black people in the US have higher rates of chronic conditions, such as diabetes and hypertension, and shorter life expectancy than their White counterparts."[5]

The most publicized discrepancy between Black and White Americans concerns the criminal justice system. A Black person in the United States is five times more likely to be pulled over by the police without just cause than a White person.[6] On average, Black men in the United States receive prison sentences 19.1 percent longer than

---

[2] "All About SAT Scores: National Average and Full Statistics," Best Colleges, accessed December 19, 2023, https://www.bestcolleges.com/research/average-sat-score-full-statistics/.

[3] "2015–16 Civil Rights Data Collection: School Climate and Safety," US Department of Education, Office of Civil Rights, May 2019, https://www2.ed.gov/about/offices/list/ocr/docs/school-climate-and-safety.pdf.

[4] "Black Women's Maternal Health," National Partnership for Women and Families, November 2023, https://www.nationalpartnership.org/our-work/health/reports/black-womens-maternal-health.html.

[5] See "Summary Health Statistics: National Health Interview Survey: 2018 (Table A-4a)," Centers for Disease Control and Prevention, November 5, 2019, https://www.cdc.gov/nchs/nhis/shs/tables.htm; "Life Expectancy at Birth, at Age 65, and at Age 75, by Sex, Race, and Hispanic Origin: United States, Selected Years 1900–2016," Centers for Disease Control and Prevention, 2017, https://www.cdc.gov/nchs/data/hus/2017/015.pdf; "Trends in Health Care Use among Black and White Persons in the US, 1963–2019," National Library of Medicine, June 14, 2022, https://www.ncbi.nlm.nih.gov/pmc/articles/PMC9198752/#abstract-a.k.b.aatitle.

[6] "Criminal Justice Fact Sheet," National Association for the Advancement of Colored People, accessed May 23, 2024, https://naacp.org/resources/criminal-justice-fact-sheet#:~:text=A%20Black%20person%20is%20five,cause%20than%20a%20Black%20woman.

White men in the United States convicted for the same crimes.[7] Black Americans and White Americans use illegal drugs at similar rates, but Black Americans are six times more likely to be arrested for drug use than White Americans.[8]

Whether one looks through the lens of economics, education, health care, or the justice system, the same inequality exists between White and Black Americans. Many of these inequalities may be traced back to the disparities created in Colonial America, but if one seeks a more recent explanation, one need go back in time no further than 1944, the year President Franklin Delano Roosevelt signed the Servicemen's Readjustment Act, more commonly known as the G.I. Bill. The G.I. Bill aimed to help veterans of World War II prosper after the war by offering low-cost mortgages, low-interest loans to start businesses, one year of unemployment compensation, and money to pay for tuition and living expenses to attend college to honorably discharged veterans who had been on active duty during the war for at least ninety days. The G.I. Bill helped usher in the greatest era of prosperity in US history. The so-called "greatest generation" came home from the war and built the United States into a superpower, largely as a result of the benefits from the G.I. Bill. Black veterans, however, did not benefit from the bill nearly as much as their White counterparts.

Language in the G.I. Bill did not specifically exclude Black veterans, but White politicians, bankers, and community leaders found ways to exclude Black veterans from receiving most of the benefits. To begin with, Black soldiers, under the leadership of White officers, received dishonorable discharges from the military at a much higher rate (39 percent compared to only 21 percent for White soldiers), thereby disqualifying them from the benefits of the G.I. Bill.[9] Additionally, Mississippi

---

[7] "Demographics Differences in Sentencing," US Sentencing Commission, November 14, 2017, https://www.ussc.gov/research/research-reports/demographic-differences-sentencing.

[8] "Criminal Justice Fact Sheet," National Association for the Advancement of Colored People, accessed May 22, 2024, https://www.naacp.org/criminal-justice-fact-sheet/.

[9] Paula S. Rothenberg, *Race, Class, and Gender in the United States: An Integrated Study*, 7th ed. (Worth, 2007), 46.

Congressman John Rankin, chair of the House Committee on Veterans' Affairs, insisted that individual states administer the benefits instead of the federal government. This decision ensured that local and state politicians, as well as bankers and other community leaders, could create unfair systems to exclude many Black veterans from receiving most of the benefits. Black veterans were denied mortgage loans from White-controlled banks, denied tuition dollars to attend four-year colleges (and were denied admission altogether to most Southern colleges and universities), denied the right to build houses in most middle-class neighborhoods, and denied loans to build houses or start businesses in certain parts of town.[10]

Some White Americans might reason, "Jim Crow is over, and everyone has the same opportunities now. We should just quit talking about slavery, segregation, and racism, and move forward together." Such statements, however, ignore the generational poverty created and sustained by slavery, Jim Crow segregation, and numerous other laws designed to give White citizens an unfair advantage. Even though most of those laws no longer exist, their legacies will continue to impact Black individuals and households in the United States for generations to come. The preceding paragraphs provide evidence that work still remains in the fight for racial equality in the United States. If White women and men indeed care about racial equality, and if they really feel such a strong bond with those who marched, protested, and agitated for civil rights in the middle decades of the twentieth century, they should know that the struggle continues today.

In the twenty-first century, numerous Church of Christ leaders are following in the footsteps of Carl Spain, Walter Burch, John Allen Chalk, Dwain Evans, and Bud Stumbaugh. During the summer of 2018,

---

[10] Erin Blakemore, "How the GI Bill's Promise was Denied to a Million Black WWII Veterans," *History*, June 21, 2023, https://www.history.com/news/gi-bill-black-wwii-veterans-benefits; Les Picker, "The G.I. Bill, World War II, and the Education of Black Americans," National Bureau of Economic Research, *The Digest* (Dec. 2002): 4; Louis Lee Woods II, "Almost 'No Negro Veteran . . . Could Get a Loan': African Americans, the GI Bill, and the NAACP Campaign against Residential Segregation, 1917–60," *The Journal of African American History* 98, no. 3 (2013): 392–417.

Ron Holland, retired minister at The Hills Church in Fort Worth, Texas, wrote a book titled *Let's Talk Race: A Beginner's Guide to Conversations about Race.* This book provided a skeleton for a four-week class designed to "prepare White people to be able to have meaningful conversations about race in a multiracial/multiethnic environment."[11] Not long after its inception, Holland's daughter, Shelley Park, took the reins of LTR [Let's Talk Race] Ministries, a nonprofit organization that aims to help "White people and predominantly white churches begin the journey of racial reconciliation."[12] She serves as president of that organization, and her husband, David, serves as vice president. As of 2024, more than one thousand White members of Churches of Christ have completed the Let's Talk Race curriculum.

The Carl Spain Center on Race Studies and Spiritual Action began in 2018 on the campus of Abilene Christian University under the leadership of Jerry Taylor. The Center seeks to foster racial unity within Churches of Christ and its affiliated institutions.[13] Since its beginning, the Center has hosted numerous Racial Unity Leadership Summits across the United States, bringing together Black and White denominational leaders to study, worship, and build relationships with one another. The organization also has organized rallies against racism, hosted special lectures on the topics of race and racism, established a scholarship for Black students to attend Abilene Christian University, and even led multiday bus trips for White and Black denominational members to visit important civil rights movement sites together.[14] The Carl Spain Center also has spawned other organizations, including MARCH, a diverse group of ministers in the Dallas–Fort Worth area who meet regularly "to build strong genuine Christ-centered

---

[11] "Our Story," Let's Talk Race, accessed May 23, 2024, https://ltrministries.com/About?scrollTo=Story.

[12] "Our Story," Let's Talk Race.

[13] Carl Spain Center on Race Studies and Spiritual Action, accessed May 23, 2024, https://carlspaincenter.org/.

[14] Greg Jaklewicz, "'Hard Truths' Directed to Those Gathered at Abilene Christian's Community Rally," *Abilene Reporter-News*, June 7, 2020.

relationships that go beyond our social divisions of race, class, or gender."[15] The leaders of Let's Talk Race and the Carl Spain Center add their voices to the courageous leaders from the 1960s who risked their reputations, income, and safety to challenge racism in all its forms.

This book also attempts to add a voice to the chorus of civil rights activists from previous generations, or, at the very least, allow the voices from the past to be heard above the sheer silence. The picture painted of twentieth-century Churches of Christ displays the racism of N. B. Hardeman and Foy Wallace Jr., the deafness of Reuel Lemmons and B. C. Goodpasture, and the silence of James Fowler in bold and colorful strokes, but it leaves out Spain, Burch, Chalk, Evans, Stumbaugh, and many others who raised their voices in protest. The present volume seeks to lift their stories from obscurity, thereby granting them their proper and esteemed places in the narrative and allowing people to see a fuller and more accurate picture of Church of Christ history. Their lives demand attention. Not only do their stories contribute to a more accurate picture of history, but they also provide courage to present-day civil rights activists.

Slavery often bears the monicker of "original sin," and although slavery ended after the Civil War, it continues to negatively affect US citizens through unequal opportunities for economic uplift, housing, healthcare, and education. More obvious than these inequalities is the racial tension that always exists just beneath the surface of the American landscape. Just as magma always exists below the crust of the Earth, not visible to humans walking on the surface, racism flows beneath the culture of the United States—always present although often invisible to many US citizens. On occasion, magma erupts onto the surface through violent volcanos, causing a destructive force that melts everything in its path. The racism flowing beneath the American landscape also erupts on occasion, becoming visible in violent and destructive ways for everyone to see. Racism erupted during the era of the Civil War, the bloodiest

---

[15] "About Us," MARCH Dallas, https://marchdallas.org/aboutus/.

and most deadly conflict in US history. Racism erupted during the Civil Rights Movement, allowing US citizens (South and North) to see the visible manifestations of hate and bigotry in the streets of Birmingham, Selma, and Montgomery.

In the opening decades of the twenty-first century, racism has erupted again. On February 26, 2013, a seventeen-year-old Black teenager named Trayvon Martin was shot dead on the streets of Sanford, Florida, by George Zimmerman, who said the teenager looked suspicious. Initially, Zimmerman faced no charges at all, and later, a jury acquitted him on charges of second-degree murder and manslaughter. Martin's death sparked national debate, outrage, and violence. On August 9, 2014, Ferguson police officer Darren Wilson shot and killed an unarmed Black man named Michael Brown. That event sparked the so-called Ferguson uprising, which included three distinct waves of riots on the streets of that St. Louis suburb. On September 6, 2018, Botham Jean, a Black member of Churches of Christ, sat alone in his apartment in Dallas when Amber Guyger, an off-duty police officer, entered his apartment and fatally shot him. Although eventually charged with murder, Guyger was initially charged only with manslaughter, sparking protests and riots in the streets once again. On May 25, 2020, Derek Chauvin, a Minneapolis police officer, murdered George Floyd, another unarmed Black man, on the streets of that city, and a bystander recorded the crime, making that racist act visible to the world. Following Floyd's death, protests erupted throughout all fifty states and internationally. To this list could be added scores of other racially motivated clashes, including the deadly shooting at Emanuel African Methodist Episcopal Church in Charleston, South Carolina, in 2015; the riots that occurred in the streets of Baltimore after the death of Freddie Gray in 2015; and the violence that followed the 2016 shooting and killing of Keith Lamont Scott in Charlotte. Not since the days of the civil rights movement has racism appeared so vividly to the American public.

When protesters hit the streets in the 1960s, many White citizens immediately found ways to criticize their efforts, calling them troublemakers, outsiders, Communists, and atheists. Instead of listening to prophetic calls for justice, those individuals resorted to name-calling and found ways to discredit the prophets. As Black (and White) Americans once again protest racism in its many forms a half-century following the civil rights movement, many White voices have resorted to those historic patterns. Instead of heeding the most important messages of Black Lives Matter activists and those protesting racially motivated police brutality, some White Americans seek only to discredit and demean the messengers. Instead of joining the outcries to treat all humans as beings made in the image of God, some White Christians continue to hand ownership of these important conversations to politicians at the state and federal levels. If these Christians believe God remains sovereign over all things, one wonders why they have labeled select, consequential conversations (especially those pertaining to the dignity and equality of human beings) off-limits for preachers and church leaders to discuss inside the church building.

Once again, not unlike the turbulent decade of the 1960s, White preachers face backlash from their congregations and church leaders for broaching the topics of social justice or race from the pulpit. From this volume, readers should especially note that virtually all courageous White leaders within Churches of Christ who raised their voices against the racist status quo in the 1960s were forced into silence through violence, intimidation, or termination. After 1960, Carl Spain never publicly addressed the topic of racism again. By the end of the 1960s, White Churches of Christ had so marginalized Walter Burch that his voice barely remained audible. John Allen Chalk left congregational ministry less than two years following his bold statements on the three American revolutions. Bud Stumbaugh lasted only five years in ministry and still endured the agony of being fired from two separate congregations and the emotional stress of receiving threats to his safety and his life. The Bible and history bear witness that speaking courageous words from God is not for the faint of heart, and present-day church leaders should support (rather than challenge) the prophets who dare to raise their voices against injustice.

In such a racially charged climate, what role should the church play? Perhaps instead of name-calling, people of faith should take a page from Spain's book and speak boldly and courageously on behalf of those who find themselves without an advocate. Instead of seeking ways to discredit every messenger of difficult-to-hear messages, perhaps followers of God should follow in the footsteps of Burch, who spent much of his life bringing Black and White people together to discuss racial healing, orchestrating their voices to promote racial harmony. Instead of aligning ourselves with one political party over another in discussions about race and racism, perhaps the church should listen to the voice of Chalk, the Abilene-based herald who used the radio and the pulpit to frame his message of racial reconciliation around Scripture instead of politics. Instead of joining the masses and multitudes who contribute to the extreme polarization in US society, perhaps Christ followers should join the chorus of Christ followers who came before us, including Evans and Stumbaugh, who sought true peace, the peace of God, by speaking truth even when truth was difficult to hear. The lives and legacies of these courageous leaders remind all generations of Christians that the church has something to say about racism. The church needs only to lift its voice.

Appendices

"Negro Meetings For White People"

Foy Wallace Jr.

The manner in which the brethren in some quarters are going in for the negro meetings leads one to wonder whether they are trying to make white folks out of the negroes or negroes out of the white folks. The trend of the general mix-up seems to be toward the latter. Reliable reports have come to me of white women, members of the church, becoming so animated over a certain colored preacher as to go up to him after a sermon and shake hands with him *holding his hand in both of theirs.* That kind of thing will turn the head of most white preachers, and sometimes affect their conduct, and anybody ought to know that it will make fools out of the negroes. For any woman in the church to so far forget her dignity, and lower herself so, just because a negro has learned enough about the gospel to preach it to his race, is pitiable indeed. Her husband should take her in charge unless he has gone crazy, too. In that case somebody ought to take both of them in charge.

Reliable brethren in the Valley have reported the definite inclinations of the negro man and his wife in charge of the orphan home for colored children at Combes toward social equality. They are supposed to be members of the church, and some of the white brethren are apparently encouraging them. It is said that these two negroes have privately stated that they favor social equality and are working for it. The young editor of "Christian Soldier," in the Valley, admits that he roomed with the negro preacher, R. N. Hogan, and slept in the same bed with him two nights! And he seemed to be proud of it! Aside from being an infringement on the Jim Crow law, it is a violation of Christianity itself, and of all common decency. Such conduct forfeits the respect of right-thinking people and would be calculated to stir up demonstrations in most any community if it should become generally known.

It has gained considerable currency that the colored preacher Hogan has been too much inclined to mix with the white people and to favor, in attitude, a social equality. Hogan should have had too much sense, if not self-respect, to have permitted the young white preacher to sleep with him, if the young preacher did not have that much sense or self-respect. But Hogan has been under the sponsorship of Jimmie Lovell and cannot be expected to have any too much sense about anything. I have always said that Marshall Keeble and Luke Miller could not be spoiled, but if I ever hear of them doing anything akin to such as this I will take back every good thing I have ever said of them. Keeble should teach these negro preachers better than that, even if we cannot teach some young upstart among the white preachers. Their practices will degrade the negroes themselves. It is abominable.

When N. B. Hardeman held the Valley-wide meeting at Harlingen, Texas, some misguided brethren brought a group of negroes up to the front to be introduced to [*sic*] and shake hands with him. Brother Hardeman told them publicly that he could see all of the colored brethren he cared to see on the outside after services, and that he could say everything to them that he wanted to say without the formality of shaking hands. I think he was right. He told of a prominent brother in the church who went wild over the negroes and showed them such social courtesies that one day one of the negroes asked him if he might marry his daughter. That gave the brother a jolt and he changed his attitude!

In one of my own meetings a young negro preacher was engaged by the church as a janitor. He made it a point to stand out in the vestibule of the church-building to shake hands with the white people. When I insisted that it be discontinued some of the white brethren were offended. Such as this proves that the white brethren are ruining the negroes and defeating the very work that they should be sent to do, that is, preach the gospel to the negroes, their own people.

I saw a letter the other day from the colored preacher, R. N. Hogan, to a certain white brother stating that there were very few negroes in the section where he was preaching at the time, and that he was holding the meeting for the white brethren!

When negro meetings are held in most of the places now, the white brethren overrun the premises. They herald these negro preachers as the greatest preachers in the world, when as a matter of fact if any of the white preachers should say everything they say to a word, it would sound so common that the brethren would stop it. But when a negro says it, in negro manner, the brethren paw up the ground over it.

I was preaching in a certain city where Marshall Keeble had held a successful meeting. In usual style he had poured it on the negroes and it had run on the white people. One brother who was against *hard* preaching went wild over Keeble's hard preaching. Keeble preached it *hard*, calling names and giving the sectarians Hail Columbia! [T]his brother thought it was the greatest stuff he had ever heard. Later, when I was preaching in the same city, he squirmed until he polished the seat of a good pair of trousers because I drew the line on denominationalism. One night while he was squirming, I diverted attention by referring to one of Keeble's *hard* sayings. Immediately this brother sat erect, smiled and nodded in approval of Keeble's *hard* saying. I smiled back at him and said: Get yourself a negro preacher!

I am very much in favor of negro meetings for the negroes, but I am just as much opposed to negro meetings for white people, and I am against white brethren taking the meetings away from the negroes and the general mixing that has become entirely too much of a practice in these negro meetings. Such a thing not only lowers the church in the eyes of the world but it is definitely against the interest of the negroes. If any negro preacher says that this is not true, that will be the evidence that it is *true,* and that he has been spoiled by the white brethren and wants to preach to white audiences. And if any of the white brethren get worked up over what I have said, and want to accuse me of being jealous of the negro preachers, I will just tell them now that I don't even want to hold a meeting for any bunch of brethren who think that any negro is a better preacher than I am! So that we can just call that argument off before it starts—and the meeting, too.

—F. E. W.

"From M. Keeble"

Foy Wallace Jr.

Dear Sir and Brother in Christ:

For over thirty years I have tried to conduct my work just as your article in the *Bible Banner* of March suggested. Taking advice from such friends as you have been for years has been a blessing to my work.

So I take the privilege to thank you for that instructive and encouraging article. I hope I can conduct myself in my last days so that you and none of my friends will have to take back nothing they have said complimentary about my work or regret it.

Please continue to encourage me in my work and *pray for me*.

Fraternally yours,

M. Keeble

Wallace's Words on Keeble's Letter

This letter is characteristic of the humility of M. Keeble. It is the reason why he is the greatest colored preacher that has ever lived. Luke Miller was brought up under his teaching and has imbibed the same spirit of meekness and humility. These men know their work and do it. They know their place and stay in it, even when some white brethren try to take them out of it. I have seen Luke Miller refuse to accept places among white people that were offered to him. This is because he knows what his relationships are in the church in the light of his relationships in society.

I am still for Keeble and Miller or any other colored preacher of the gospel who has their idea of things. But I am against trying to make white folks out of the negroes or negroes out of the white folks.

"The Church And Integration"

Reuel Lemmons

The social and political question of integration has been boiling for generations. Within recent years it has reached explosive proportions. As in all other questions there are a number of brethren who are sure they know how to solve the problem of integration. They are dead sure they are right and that all others are prejudiced and unchristian. And they do not hesitate to say so. And they want it printed. We have received scores of articles on the subject of integration, both pro and con. Up until now we have not printed any of them. We think our reasons for not doing so were legitimate.

In this week's paper we are publishing two articles. We do not now intend to publish any more soon. And while we are at it we feel a few things need to be said from an editorial standpoint. Many of the most positive among the writing brethren on this subject have not lived long enough yet to know enough about the many and deep-rooted aspects of this problem to be as positive as they propose to be.

It would do good if all would carefully restudy the scriptures regarding the nature of the church. Christianity and the church were neither planned in heaven nor commissioned on Earth to revolutionize existing governments nor to uproot social structures. Rather, Christianity was designed to live and to flourish under any kind of government. Governments do not exist more tyrannical nor corrupt than was the government of Rome, and moral climate was never more adverse than in the Greek world. The church was (and is) in the world; but it was not of the world.

Slavery was an accepted norm of the first century. Slavery had nothing to do with integration so far as race is concerned, but it did have to do with integration so far as caste is concerned. There are many types of segregation and they are caused by various things—language, culture, social status, race and even occupation—for Paul segregated himself to live with Acquila [*sic*] and Priscilla because they were tent makers and so was he. He felt he had not sinned by so segregating himself. Even the Lord went off into the desert alone. The world will continue to have its segregation problems long after all of us do-gooders have passed on. Segregative practices will never be legislated out of existence. Some may, but others will arise. And brethren who fight one practice will be the first to practice another.

We do not believe that segregation has ever been a problem with the Lord's church. In my lifetime I remember only one man, in my early childhood, who would deny any human being the right to enter the kingdom of God. I know many thousands of brethren, but only one who was "off" on this point. Name any other religious question under heaven and I believe I can name more brethren who are "off" on it than on this one. It is universally believed among us that "in every nation, those who fear God and work righteousness are acceptable unto him." And certainly if they are acceptable to God they are acceptable to us. Since the day of Pentecost we have had integration in the kingdom of heaven and have believed in it. If that were not true we would not send missionaries to others. We go to men of every race and of every caste and of every vocation with the gospel, offering them the same terms and the same promises and when they accept the gospel we count them our brothers. The kingdom of heaven is the most completely integrated institution we know, and all the brethren accept all the brethren as brethren. We have never had a problem here.

There are social relationships between people who are brethren in the Lord that may present problems. Some of these problems have a valid basis and some do not. When Paul segregated himself from Barnabas at the beginning of his second missionary journey we believe he had a right to do so. We do not think it was a sin, and, somehow, we can't help but be glad that some of our brethren are not there to set the old fellow straight on this matter of integration.

On the other hand, when segregation springs from pride, vainglory, sophistication, or any other sinful characteristic it cannot be defended. Really it is but then the result of these other sins, and when we attack the symptom rather than the disease we can hardly expect to cure it. It doesn't render the rattlesnake harmless to cut off its rattles; the poison is at the other end. Paul withstood Peter because of Peter's segregation of himself from the Gentiles.

Segregation is not a "Southern problem," nor is it a modern one. Neither is it limited to a color line. The thing that pains us most is that those who know the least about it are the ones who always have the answers. They are like children—smartest at the age of four and seventeen. At four they know all the questions and at seventeen they know all the answers. Any problem regarding human rights has two sides and the ignoring of either side will bring nothing but heartache.

"Modern Challenges to Christian Morals"

Carl Spain

In this discourse we are using the word "challenge" in its original meaning. It is derived from the Latin "calumnia," meaning to defy, to falsely accuse, to deny, and contest. Serious challenges are being hurled at the defenders of the morals of the Christian faith, the faith once for all delivered to the saints and faithfully recorded in the New Testament, the only book on Christian ethics which has the divine imprimatur of our heavenly Father.

"Moral" Defined

Our English word "moral" is derived from the Latin "mores," meaning "custom," "manners," "habits." The Latin "mores" is akin to the Greek "ethos," from which we get our word "ethics." We are accustomed to making a clear distinction between the "religious" and the "moral" areas of human behavior. We recognize the validity of such a distinction in our efforts to communicate with each other in modern terminology. However, I feel that there is something vital in the import of the words of the Spirit, as they are employed in God's message to man through Christ and the New Testament revelation of truth.

We are accustomed to thinking of the "moral" as pertaining to man's relationship with man, and the "religious" as pertaining to man's relationship with God. A study of the two words as used in the Scriptures reveals a very important truth concerning Christian faith and morals. The words which pertain to "religion" have much moral meaning and value. And the words used in reference to "ethics" or "morals" sometimes have "religious" meaning and value.

In Acts 26:5 Paul speaks of "the straightest sect of our religion" (*threskos*). James uses the same word (*threskos*) when he says: "If any man thinketh himself to be religious, while he bridleth not his tongue . . . this man's religion is vain. Pure religion and undefiled before our God and Father is this, to visit the fatherless and widows in their affliction and to keep oneself unspotted from the world" (James 1:26, 27).

In the New Testament, religion is related to the moral life of the Christian. Even the true worship of God is related to the moral life of God's child. In Romans 12:1 the Spirit says to the Christian: "Present your bodies a living sacrifice, holy, acceptable to God which is your spiritual service." The word "service" is from a Greek word meaning "worship." We honor and reverence God, and show our devotion, by offering our lives daily in service to others to the glory of God (1 John 3:16). Religion that is unrelated to moral conduct is "vain," and worship that is not related to life in social or moral situations is not true worship of God. This is not the "social gospel," but it is the gospel with real social and moral emphasis.

One of the Bible words for "religion" is *eusebeia*, meaning piety, reverence, and godliness. Sometimes it is used with reference to piety toward the divine being (e.g. Acts 7:23), and again it is used in reference to piety toward our fellowman, as in 1 Timothy 5:4: "If any widow hath children, or grandchildren, let them learn first to show piety towards their own family, and to requite their parents: for this is acceptable in the sight of God."

Christian "faith" and "morals" are vitally related to each other. You cannot have one without the other. Some systems of ethics are irreligious from the Christian viewpoint. Some systems of religion are unethical from the Christian viewpoint. I find it impossible to consider Christian ethics apart from what we usually term the "religious faith" of true Christianity. The relationship is so essential, we repeat, that even the Bible word for "manners" and "customs" and "morals" is sometimes given a religious value, and the Bible word for "religion" is given a moral content.

Christian Faith and Morals

The Christian endeavors earnestly to walk by faith in moral and religious matters. He believes that there is but "one faith" (Eph. 4:5). But it is clear, from the Roman letter, that there are two aspects of the Christian faith. In Romans 10:17 the Spirit testifies that "faith cometh by hearing and hearing by the word of God." In the context the faith here referred to is to being proclaimed with urgency and insistency and shared with others to the salvation of every man's soul. But in Romans 14 the Spirit also testifies that there is an area of conscience and conviction which is not determined by a "thus saith the Lord." There is an area of "faith" which concerns Christian morals which God has not regulated by revelation. When God speaks on a moral issue, the faithful Christian listens and does the will of the Lord as He has revealed it. In moral matters there is an area determined by the mind of God as He has expressly revealed it. But there is another area which God has not bound by an express revelation of His will, which is determined by the culture in which we live and by the conscience of those whom we are seeking to save.

In Romans 14 the Spirit moved Paul's pen to write concerning the aspect of Christian faith that pertains to "scruples" (Rom. 14:1). After a discussion concerning "scruples" about matters on which God has not legislated, Paul said: "The faith which thou hast, have thou to thyself before God . . . He that doubteth is damned . . . whatsoever is not of faith is sin" (Rom. 14:22, 23).

In light of what has been said, we conclude that the Christian faith and conscience is regulated by two things: (1) What God has spoken on the issue. This area we usually describe by the phrase "bound in heaven" (Matt. 16:19). (2) The culture pattern in which we live with other people and the conscience of the unsaved with whom we mingle day by day. This is the area of faith and morals which we usually designate as "loosed in heaven" (Matt. 16:19).

In this area of faith and morals the Christian remembers the words of the Spirit in 1 Corinthians 10:23–33, where we find that there are areas of conscience and conviction which are determined by the social situation in which we live. There are some things from which Christians abstain, not because God has said "Thou shalt not," but "for conscience's sake: conscience, I say, not thine own, but the other's" (1 Cor. 10:28, 29). To this rule some may ask as Paul did, "Why is my liberty judged by another conscience? If I partake with thankfulness, why am I evil spoken of . . ." (1 Cor. 10:29, 30). To which Paul answers: "Give no occasion of stumbling . . . even as I also please all men in all things, not seeking mine own . . ." (1 Cor. 10 :32, 33).

In moral matters the Christian seeks first to please God. Secondly, he seeks to please others. Where the will of God conflicts with the will of others, he chooses to please God, and in so doing truly bless others. Where the will of God and the will of others do not conflict, he pleases God by pleasing them. In this way the Christian finds his own true happiness.

The True Basis of Morality

The naturalist contends for a morality that is based on human nature. The atheistic naturalist believes in a natural morality that has been developing within human nature through millions of years. The theistic naturalist believes in an instinctive morality that was planted in man and which works without supernatural guidance and is based on intuition rather than revelation.

We cannot be certain as to the exact measure of moral instinct which man possesses by virtue of the fact that he was created in God's image. To what extent has the sin of Adam and the sin of the human race marred that image? How much basis is there in human nature for Christian morality? To what extent is human nature morally inclined?

It is evident that man from the beginning, as recorded in Genesis, possessed a capacity for a high level of spiritual and moral conduct. But it is also evident from the beginning and before man sinned that God taught him on certain basic moral issues which man would not have known instinctively and which human nature would not have known had God not spoken. There is grave danger that our interpretation of "nature" in Romans 2 may involve us in ethical contradictions. Notice Romans 2:13–15:

> Gentiles that have not the law do by nature the things of the law, these not having the law, are the law unto themselves, in that they show the works of the law written in their hearts, their conscience bearing witness therewith, and their thoughts one with another accusing or else excusing them.

Before we conclude how much of the law the Gentiles did by nature, let us remember that Paul also said:

> How be it, I had not known sin, except through the law: for I had not known coveting, except the law had said, Thou shalt not covet . . . For we know that law is spiritual: but I am carnal, sold under sin . . . For I know that in me, that is, in my flesh, dwelleth no good thing: for to will is present with me, but to do that which is good is not (Rom. 7:7, 8, 14, 18).

In the above passages the Holy Spirit makes it right clear that human nature alone is incapable of Christian morality and needs divine help and guidance. This is especially true since sin entered the experience of the human race, and death by sin. But there is good evidence that Adam and Eve, even before the fall, needed instruction in righteousness. A quick glance at the inspired account of man's fellowship with God, before sin disturbed that fellowship, will bear this out. Carl F. H. Henry suggests:

> Even though Adam had a certain morality written into his nature, there was still need for specific instruction and

commandments conveyed externally by supernatural disclosure. In man's primal state the basic elements of morality that were his by creation were insufficient to define the whole content of human duty. His spiritual nature doubtless bound man to act in the spirit of truth and right, but he could not derive all the commandments of a dutiful life from his inner constitution. The Genesis account contradicts any idea that the law engraved on man's heart gave him detailed content from which he could deduce every factor of the moral claim.

In our interpretation of "nature" in Romans 2:14 we must not contradict what Paul says in Romans 7. If the Jews could not fully know the moral law of Moses by natural instinct, or by innate conscience, then we must not conclude that the Gentiles could.

But, in any event, it is evident from the book of Romans that neither Gentile nor Jew could attain unto the lofty plain of Christian ethics without leaving the level of ethics based on human nature and rising to the level of ethics based on divine nature. Simon Peter stated it precisely and concisely when he said:

> Seeing that his divine power hath granted unto us all things that pertain unto life and godliness, through the knowledge of him that called us to glory and virtue; whereby he hath granted unto us his precious and exceeding great promises; that through these ye may become partakers of the divine nature, having escaped the corruption that is in the world by lust. (2 Pet. 1:3, 4)

Jesus Himself said: "Except a man be born anew, he cannot see the kingdom of God" (John 3:3). This means literally "born from above." Our Lord continued by saying: "Except a man be born of water and the Spirit, he cannot enter the kingdom of God. That which is born of flesh is flesh; and that which is born of the Spirit is spirit" (John 3:5, 6).

Without exception, the New Testament teaching concerning Christian morality is based on the fact that Christians are children of

God by virtue of a new birth. As Paul reasons with the Corinthians about the level of their moral attitudes and conduct, he bases his plea on the fact that they are children of God and are partakers of the divine nature. He reminded them that "the natural man receiveth not the things of the Spirit of God: for they are foolishness unto him; and he cannot know them for they are spiritually judged" (1 Cor. 2:14). Then the apostle moves on to moral principles based on the love of God as demonstrated in Christ, and he reaches his grand conclusion in 1 Corinthians 16:14: "Let all that you do be done in love!"

Likewise the apostle John, dealing with the lofty principles of Christian ethics in 1 John, starts out in the very beginning by establishing the true basis and source of Christian morality in the nature of God, whose children we are. Because we are partakers of God's nature, our moral standards are based on the proposition that God's nature is imparted to His children. This most certainly has moral implications and consequences in his dealings with his fellow man.

The "Golden Rule" or "Royal Law"

The relationship between Christian morality and the divine nature is set forth very clearly in the word of God. In the past I have thought that the highest level of morality was expressed in the language that we often refer to as "The Golden Rule." I was shocked when I discovered that this was the law and the prophets before Jesus lived and died. "All things therefore whatsoever ye would that men should do unto you, even so do ye unto them: for this is the law and the prophets" (Matt. 7:12).

In the same sermon Jesus said: "Ye therefore shall be perfect, as your heavenly Father is perfect." The Apostle Paul by the Spirit adds his witness:

> Owe no man anything, save to love one another: for he that loveth his neighbor hath fulfilled the law. For this, Thou shalt not commit adultery, Thou shalt not kill, Thou shalt not steal, Thou shalt not covet, and if there be any other commandment, . . . is summed up in this word namely, Thou shalt love

thy neighbor as thyself. Love worketh no ill to his neighbor:
love therefore is the fulfillment of the law. (Rom. 13:8–10)

Then, Paul adds a few verses later: "Put ye on the Lord Jesus Christ." He goes on to give "love" the new content of the New Testament and makes of it a new commandment (compare 1 John 2:7, 8) by giving it a fuller and richer meaning.

The word "Golden" still applies to the ethics of the law and prophets. It is also the Royal Law of James 2:8. It is still a royal law that is part of the new commandment of the New Testament. When the mathematician moves from algebra, trigonometry, and geometry into calculus, he does not throw the former into the waste basket, but jealously cherishes it so that he may build upon it and reach to loftier heights. He doesn't even dare throw away his multiplication table.

It is tragic that Christians have such difficulty living up to the law and prophets in the life of love. But it is even more tragic that we have not walked on higher ground, "having been begotten again, not of corruptible seed, but of incorruptible, through the word of God which liveth and abideth" (1 Pet. 1:23). As new creatures, born of God, we have purified our souls in obedience to the truth unto unfeigned love of the brethren, and are called upon to "love one another with a pure heart fervently" (1 Pet. 1:22).

Paul concludes his great book on love with these words: "Let all that you do be done in love" (1 Cor. 16:14). The book of 1 Corinthians is a great book, more than just chapter 13, on the practical ethics of Christian love. No one can really understand 1 Corinthians 13 without reading the entire book, because it is in the book itself that the new content of the new commandment is really defined.

Paul moves beyond the law and the prophets on the Golden Rule and gives love its new content when he says: "Be ye therefore imitators of God as dear children. And walk in love as Christ also hath loved us" (Eph. 5:1, 2). Jesus Himself said to His disciples: "Love one another as I have loved you" (John 15:12).

The Jewish Spirit of Anti-Christ

Modern antagonism toward the ethics of Jesus is inseparably identified with the denial of His Divine Sonship. One basic reason why men deny His divinity is the fact that they do not agree with His moral attitude. The Nazi and Communist and Jew have one thing in common: they all despise the ethics of Jesus.

Representative of the spirit of anti-Christ among many modern Jews is Rabbi Joseph Klausner. In his book, *Jesus of Nazareth*, he hurls his blasphemous indictments against our Lord. It all adds up to the bold accusation that the morals of Jesus are unworthy of the respect of decent people.

The Rabbi hurls his challenge on the following counts. We will do no more than state them. You who know Jesus, and who understand the moral and religious and political conditions of the Greek, Roman–Jewish world in which Jesus lived, will make your own reply in your own enlightened hearts:

1. The Rabbi says that Jesus abstracted religion and ethics from the rest of social life, in His efforts to establish a kingdom not of this world.

2. He accuses Jesus of rashly setting aside all the requirements of the national life in an effort to set up an ethico-religious system based on His own perverted conception of the Godhead.

3. Jesus, he says, ignored the religious and national culture in His effort to abolish it, rather than seeking to reform and improve the nation's knowledge, art, and culture.

4. Jesus, says the Rabbi, invited social chaos by substituting the foolish principle of nonresistance for civil justice. In this respect, the Rabbi stumbles over the Cross of Christ.

5. According to Klausner, Jesus took no interest in labor, or in political and economic achievement, and foolishly recommended the "unanxious, toilless life of the birds and lilies"!

6. Jesus, he accuses, ignored the requirements of distributive justice by refusing to become a judge or divider in the case of the man who said "bid my brother divide the inheritance with me."
7. Jesus, according to the Jewish Rabbi, ignored everything concerned with material civilization.

Having hurled these and other challenges, he concludes that the Jewish nation was very wise in rejecting Jesus of Nazareth, and he adds, "two thousand years of non-Jewish Christianity have proved that the Jewish people did not err."

It is a fact that Nazism and Communism have been viciously Anti-Semitic in our century. How strange it is that the Semitic-Anti-Christ and the Anti-Semitic Anti-Christ join hands, like Herod and Pilate, and become ethical friends when they face the question: "What, then, shall we do with Jesus?"

Rabbi Klausner defends the Jewish nation against Jesus with the same charge that the atheist Celsus brought against Christians in defense of the Roman Empire. Christians were accused of contributing to the fall of the empire by their lack of concern for Rome's materialistic defense and reconstruction. In modern times Marx and Lenin have accused Christians of showing too little concern for life on Earth, and too much concern for life eternal. The death cries of millions under the Anti-Christ rule of Communism give ringing evidence that Christians have good reason to give much thought to the life hereafter. The only alternative for men of honor is to bear a cross instead of a sword. The sword will only spread the destructive disease of greed and hate. The cross burns in a healing way and destroys the disease without destroying the person.

The Challenge of Modern Naturalism

The subject of morality is being diligently studied by modern atheists who deny the existence of God. On the basis of logical materialism they deny the Christian doctrine of divine revelation and regeneration. Many distinct and conflicting ethical systems have marched under the banner of logical materialism. Outstanding among them in our time are the advocates of Behaviorism with its emphasis on naturalistic morality in an atheistic society. According to this theory of morals, man is not responsible for any of his actions. What he does or says or thinks at any given moment is the result of chemical and physical forces within his own physical nature and in the physical world around him. He cannot do right or wrong because these natural forces determine his choice, and he, of his own free will, really has no choice. If man cannot choose, he has no choice. If he has no choice, he is not responsible for his actions. Behaviorism is one of the modern Goliaths who hurls his atheistic challenge at the children of God. He stands with arrogant confidence, trusting in his materialistic armor. He laughs at the Christian soldier who stands with no shield—Goliath cannot see the shield of faith that only faith can see. Behaviorism boasts its scientific attitude and has good reason to be embarrassed, because there is no scientific proof that consciousness or conscience is nothing but physical and electrical motion.

Among those of Naturalistic persuasion there are those who keep company with Marx and Lenin, marching under the standard of the camp of Dialectical (Logical) Materialism and Political Naturalism. They, too, are atheistic and Anti-Christ. Reviving the ancient philosophy of Plato's Republic, and adding a modern flavor with the pen of Marx and Lenin, they have marched in arrogant pomp and pride in the spirit of Friedrich Nietzsche under the banner of Nazism, raping the land and the people of Belgium, Norway, Czechoslovakia, and Poland. Then the circumstances reversed as "Beelzebub cast out Beelzebub," and the Marxian Communist, with the spirit of Lenin and lead by Stalin, marched back through Poland and the other countries that had been tortured by the Nazis. They slaughtered and imprisoned "naive, simple-minded Christians" who could not fight back because they were under the influence of the opiate of pure and undefiled religion! And, under the Communist banner, they continued to march with giant strides across China and Korea and even now cast a black shadow over the borders of India, breathing threatening and slaughter with the spirit of Anti-Christ. The Communist Manifesto of Karl Marx lived on in the heart of Lenin and reached Goliath stature in the Machiavellian ethics of Stalin. This same spirit of political naturalism also found expression in the twentieth century in Mussolini of Italy. And in our own beloved America, under the banner of white supremacy, it marches with burning crosses across our nation cursing the doctrine that all men are born free and equal. Robed in the un-American garb of the Ku Klux Klan, or in the robes of governors and senators and legislators it intimidates and legislates with utter contempt for Christ who sits as Judge in the Highest Court of Appeals in questions concerning the bill of human rights.

Political naturalism has as many faces as Nikita Khrushchev. It wears one face in the corrupt political and religious pressure groups in our country. It wears another face in Russia, and still another in China. Its beastly character takes the form of a Bear or a Dragon. It becomes a wolf in sheep's clothing, piously pronouncing the name of Christ with the tongue of Khrushchev, who added insult to injury when he replied to Mr. Skourzo, a Greek immigrant in Hollywood: "The Greeks and the Russians are brothers in Christ!" To such atheistic politicians, evil is good when it accomplishes one's goal, and good is evil when it obstructs their path to power. It is the philosophy of Plato, who insisted that the superior, stronger man has the right to get the advantage of the inferior, weaker man. It is right and good for the most powerful to legislate in their own interest.

Whether we are willing to admit it or not, there are some dark chapters in the history of America in which are recorded deeds of Political Naturalism as vile as have ever been perpetrated on the face of the Earth. Marching under the standard of the god of mammon and bluffing his way with ballots and bullets, the white man put his big white foot on the Negro's neck, quoted the pledge of allegiance to the flag, and piously recited platitudes about all men being born free and equal.

What right have we to talk about the two faces of Khrushchev, when we guard the ballot boxes with guns and pass laws that deny native Americans the right to vote on the basis of their color and social background? Like Khrushchev, many Americans just don't agree with Jesus about His moral code. The ethics of Jesus are foolish to many church goers.

I shall never forget how Christ was crucified by "His own" in a southern community where I grew up. A few law-abiding, humble-hearted Negroes wanted to attend a service of the church of Christ. They had listened to me preach on the radio. These souls didn't know anything about an organization for the advancement of colored people. They traded with my beloved step-father, who seemed to be interested in their souls. They loved him like a mongrel dog would love a man who fed him and spoke kindly to him when he was accustomed to being cursed and kicked.

When our colored friends timidly asked if they could attend a service of the white folks and learn more about the church of Christ, I made the mistake of telling them that they would be more than welcome. And they trusted me. They came in timidly and took the seats that were as far back as they could get and still be inside. I shall never forget the agony on their faces when white Christians made it very plain to them that they were out of place and glared at them like a Jew would have looked upon a "Samaritan dog." The Negroes left the assembly of the saints. It seemed that the saints couldn't pray or sing just right as long as there were "niggers" in the church house.

A few years later, the Negroes of the community got to hear the gospel from a man of their own race. But the Lord didn't seem to understand about the white folks' problem, or if He did, He didn't seem to care. And the gospel seed that a white man had sown in the Negro heart was watered to life by a Negro preacher. And the Lord gave the increase, but He didn't time it just right. He forgot that the poor Negro folks who were to be baptized didn't have anything but a tent, and the white folks had the only available baptistry. So, in the excitement of becoming the white folks' brothers and sisters in the Lord, the happy preacher didn't see anything wrong about asking if they could come over and use the baptistry.

The Lord had moved in the hearts of a few white Christians in such a powerful way that they said that their Negro friends would be more than welcome. But the blue-blooded members of the Royal Order of the Master Race, including many members of the church of Christ, the Baptist, the Methodist, and Presbyterians protested violently.

They preferred death to a fate such as this. Before the baptismal service was over, police came to put a stop to it. Just like the Communists broke up services in Warsaw, Poland, last year. The local paper took up the fight in good old "Democratic" style. Police patrolled the area around the church building. The Lord's church was branded as a Communist front organization where whites and Negroes socialized as brothers. The community systematically boycotted the business establishments of some of the Christians for months, nearly causing them to go bankrupt.

I grew up in that community. I saw firsthand the kind of social paranoia that caused the Jews to hate Jesus and nail Him to a tree.

There is little to be gained by preaching against the immoral actions of Communists, unless we as Christians are willing to repent of our own idolatry and murder. The word of the Lord identifies covetousness with idolatry, and hate with murder. We have so defined "moral" and "immoral" in our modern times that a covetous idolater and hateful murderer can go to church and be in full fellowship because he doesn't smoke, chew, drink, or dance. These latter things we ought not to do, but we need to expand the borders of our moral realm and condemn certain areas that have been condoned.

In correcting social evils, we must resort to the educational approach before we attempt legislation. We must preach righteousness and educate in a Christian way before any legislation will prove effective. Education without legislation is usually more effective than legislation without education. But when people insist on using the Bible to support an un-Christian system of ethics, one can expect that social revolution will follow, with its usual attending evils. God forbid that churches of Christ, and schools operated by Christians, shall be the last stronghold of refuge for socially sick people who have Nazi illusions about the Master Race. Political naturalism, in the cloak of the Christian priesthood, must not be the ethical code in the kingdom of Jesus Christ.

I feel certain that Jesus would say: "Ye hypocrite! You say you are the only true Christians, and make up the only true church, and have the only Christian schools. Yet, you drive one of your own preachers to denominational schools where he can get credit for his work and refuse to let him take Bible for credit in your own school because the color of his skin is dark!"

Our moral attitudes are so mixed up that we use the story of Philemon and Onesimus to justify refusing a Negro admission to study Bible in our graduate school of Bible.

A Methodist college will admit our own Negro preacher brethren and give them credit for their work. Baptist colleges in Texas will do as much. Our State universities will admit them. There is no law of our State or nation that will censor us. The Bible does not rule against it. Why are we afraid? The integrated schools of San Angelo, Texas, ninety miles from Abilene, are rated at the top in our nation. Are we moral cowards on this issue? There are people with money who will back us in our last ditch stand for white supremacy in a world of pigmented people. God forbid that we shall be the last stronghold among religious schools where the politico-economic philosophy of naturalism determines our moral conduct.

We fear the mythical character named Jim Crow more than we reverence Jesus Christ. In the name of "discretion" we make un-Christian and un-American rules like some states do in the name of "State's Rights." To complacent Jews who boasted that they alone were acceptable to God, Jesus said: "Outwardly you are like whited sepulchers, but inwardly you are full of dead men's bones." Let this be a warning to any people who say they are the only Christians in the world. The surest way to seal the doom of this nation is for the only Christians to be the only ones with un-Christian attitudes.

The Pharisees of Jesus's day had developed a code of morals by which they could safely parade their piety before men. They reduced morality to certain matters like tithing mint, anise, and cumin, and "omitted the weightier matters of the law, judgment, mercy, and faith" (Matt. 23:23). "They became blind guides that strained at gnats and swallowed camels" (Matt. 23:24).

Some say it is the church, not the school, that must lead out in such matters. We have just said that education is the best approach to the solution of any problem. Our only excuse for existing as institutions of Christian education is to make better citizens of the kingdom of Christ and better citizens for service in a free society.

We reject even our own preachers, and refuse them credit for their work in Bible, on the grounds that we do not have separate facilities for them to sleep and eat. If that is the only issue, then why reject someone who doesn't ask that we provide a place for him to eat or sleep?

Brethren, we are not recommending revolutionary legislation. We are merely suggesting that we offer Christian education to all Americans without respect of persons. If the problem is one of room and board, then let us consider that we have no problem if we do not have to provide room and board.

Idealistic Ethics

Rivaling naturalism for the mastery of Western thought is idealism. Idealism asserts that man is able by rational processes to discover the good life. As there are many theories among the naturalists, even so the idealists have many theories. But all of it has led to speculative rationalism which insists that human reason has unlimited power to discover the good life without divine revelation and without a naturalistic study of sensory experiences.

Time and space do not permit a discussion of the rational idealism of Plato, Aristotle, and Hegel, nor of the Categorical Imperative and postulational idealism of Immanuel Kant. In his *Critique of Pure Reason*, Kant opposes any effort to reduce knowledge of good and evil to mere sensory perception. The idealists insist that man's knowledge extends by the power of the mind into the invisible spiritual and moral order and that by pure meditation man can furnish rational proof of the moral discoveries of the mind.

There have been three strong opponents of rational idealism in the Western world. (1) The Christian faith based on revelation of God's will in the Bible; (2) the irrational, super-naturalistic and religious naturalism of which Soren Kierkegaard is representative; and (3) the naturalistic and anti-religious systems of Karl Marx and Friedrich Nietzsche with their irrational methods of approach to the good life.

The first of these is a protest based on a faith delivered by God to man by supernatural intervention through revelation. The second and third are forerunners of modern existentialism. We shall consider the ethics of existentialism, but, before we do, let us bear in mind that two of the "founding fathers" of existential ethics were the supernaturalistic and religious Kierkegaard, and the naturalistic, anti-religious Nietzsche! Two ethical philosophies that were uncompromisingly opposed to each other have, through the fickle fellowship of modern minds, given birth to the popular philosophy of existentialism.

Many books from the popular religious press have been circulated in recent years in the Western world. Many of them have been translations of the writings of European existentialists who have been influenced by the anti-religious and religious philosophies that have influenced the thinking of Europe in the nineteenth and twentieth centuries. If existentialism perplexes one, and he finds within it seeming contradictions, he will do well to remember Kierkegaard and Nietzsche, both of whom made their contribution to existentialism.

Existential Ethics

Let us consider briefly this philosophy which repudiates all forms of systematic morality. Carl F. H. Henry's observations on existentialism are clear and concise in defining this modern moral philosophy: "Decision, rather (than reason), constitutes the warp and woof of life for existential ethics." The existentialist scorns every endeavor to define moral and spiritual claims by rational criteria. Such realities, he contends, are grasped solely by "practical–existential" decision.

It seems that in the chaos of thought in the pre-existential philosophy faith was dethroned by reason, and rationalism reigned in Western thought. The cult of rationalism paraded proudly under the influence of men like Descartes and Hegel. There was nothing in reality that man could not attain by pure reason.

Then agnosticism and evolutionary thought dethroned reason, and, under the influence of David Hume, even Kant was somewhat inhibited by the terrific impact of agnosticism. But Kant helped to prepare the world for existentialism because he, in agreement with Hume, "denied any possibility of knowing the spiritual world conceptually. Abandoning the religious grounding of morality, he oriented the discussion of ethics to the practical reason and to immanent value–experience."

Henry continues to point out certain "observable influences" that contributed to the modern existential mood:

> Both Nietzsche and Kierkegaard have made their contribu-
> tion. Whatever their differences, each repudiates the attempt
> to grasp reality rationally, and each seeks instead to do so
> from the standpoint of existence, or subjective immediacy.

Henry's observation concerning existentialism's pragmatic attitude is worthy of note: "It cuts reason off from any ontic relation to universal essences and changeless absolutes, and indeed, denies the very reality of such." This has serious implications to the Christian who accepts a divinely revealed system of moral conduct. If there is no "universal essence," there is no God who is immutable and changeless, and there are no principles that are eternal. Let Henry continue his analysis of the ethics of existentialism:

> The moral life needs no clarification of the metaphysical
> hinterland before posing the question, 'What ought I to do?'
> Such inquiries as 'What kind of a universe is this?' or 'What
> life-view is demanded by this world-view?' only divert the
> individual from the task of living passionately at the moment.
> Existentialism scorns the attempt to formulate a
> world-and-life view. . . . Thus the entire moral tradition of the

West, except for occasional strands influenced by postulational ethics, is repudiated as speculative rationalism.

The existential moralist proposes, instead, a 'practical morality.' He inquires: 'What shall I do in this concrete predicament in view of its specific alternatives?' and not, 'What is the nature of duty?' or 'What is the nature of the self that it should be required to do anything at all?' . . . In dynamic decision man creatively makes his own tomorrow in a context of existence which is neither bound by necessity nor hemmed in by reason. The problems of life are psychological, not logical. Hence ethical decision must be ventured on the existential-practical plane, rather than from the theoretical point of view.

All of this helps to explain the modern philosophies of Nazism and Communism. Friedrich Nietzsche (nineteenth century), who is admittedly one of the predecessors of existential ethics, was a younger contemporary of Karl Marx. Both were atheists and accepted the materialistic view of the universe. Nietzsche's power-ethics harmonizes with the Marxist contention that the world's greatest need is economic power. Marx believed that the only real malady of the human race is an economic one. This fits neatly into Nietzsche's theory that the ultimate reality can only be understood from the powerful forces of man's immediate environment.

Those who have jumped on the existential bandwagon will do well to remember that it was a man with an existential mood who said in his *Ecce Homo* that Christian morality is the most malignant form of all falsehood. He denounced it as poisonous, decadent, and weakening. And in his book, *A Genealogy of Morals*, the same Nietzsche said the "Golden Rule" contradicted man's natural instinct and that Jesus Christ was a seductive Jew whose Cross was a subtle means of obtaining power.

William Barrett, the author of *Irrational Man*, gives a popular definitive study of existential philosophy.

> . . . this philosophy derives from concrete and everyday
> human experience rather than from abstract or specialized
> areas of knowledge . . . Its method is to begin with this human
> existence as a fact without any ready-made preconceptions
> about the essence of man. There is no prefabricated human
> nature that freezes human possibilities into a preordained
> mold. . . . "Existence precedes essence," as the formula puts it.

Barrett also insists that the existentialists of this century are the heirs of Kierkegaard and Nietzsche. In Kierkegaard we catch the flavor of Kant's idealism, and in Nietzsche the flavor of Marxian-Lenin ethics of political and economic power.

The existential theory is espoused by theists, atheists, and agnostics with equal passion. Barrett, in defending the fact that existentialism attracts all types of ethical philosophies, writes:

> These men have different problems, attack the problems by
> different methods, and on a number of points are in disagree-
> ment. Hence some critics declared that existentialism is not
> a unified movement at all, with the implication that it may not
> even be a definite philosophy. On the contrary, a movement
> is alive and vital only when it is able to generate differences
> among its followers; when everybody agrees, we may be sure
> that it has declined into the stereotyped rigidity of death.

From the above statement we can see that the liberal mood and the existential mood are very much alike. And we are familiar with the consequences of liberalism in the social and political morals of our day, and also in the theology of modernism. There are, however, at least two moral philosophies that are not welcome in the existential house: (1) Behaviorism, with its absolute emphasis on chemical and physical forces in man and his environment in determining moral conduct, and (2) New Testament Christianity, with its emphasis on the eternal principles and definite standards of moral conduct for all ages as long as man lives on the Earth.

As long as Christians insist that the Christian ethic is revealed to us by God, an Absolute Being, through Jesus Christ, and that in Jesus we find the perfect divinity and perfect humanity, just so long Christians will find the existential fellowship an unfriendly one. And as long as we insist that the New Testament is the only book in the world on Christian faith and morals which has the imprimatur of the Spirit of the one true God and His Son Jesus Christ, just so long will we be unwelcome in the liberal fellowship of the existentialists.

To the atheistic existentialist, the absence of absolute values means unlimited and unthwarted freedom. To him the only sure thing is death. And the true meaning of life is determined by the present act alone. To the theistic existentialist, it is the philosophical spirit that should prevail in the magic moment of decision. To a theological existentialist, like Karl Barth, the magic moment of immediate decision is influenced by divine revelation, not Biblical, but a special communication from God; not from within man subjectively, but from God outside of man. The existential magic moment is determined by God Himself, who thus confronts man with the moment of decision. With another theological, revelational existentialist, Emil Brunner, there is the doctrine of a subjective "twilight knowledge" of God's will in the human conscience which speaks to man in the moment of subjective immediacy.

Even neo-orthodoxy fits into the pattern of existential ethics. This modern school of theology has developed an ethical theory which insists that Christian ethics require Christian faith. Then, as Henry puts it, neo-orthodoxy attempts: ". . . to identify revelational ethics with the existential and to repudiate the theoretical. Two important elements cut neo-orthodoxy loose from the historic Christian view of Biblical ethics. One is the rejection of propositional revelation, thus denying the rational base for theology and ethics. The other is making revelation to be an immediate encounter only. This by-passes an inspired and authoritative Scripture."

The Threat of Worldliness

No challenge to Christian morals is quite so subtle and so dangerous as that which comes from the unconverted members of the Christian fellowship itself. There are many practical atheists among us who are morally loose because they do not really believe that the Earth and the works therein shall be burned up and that they must soon stand before the judgment throne of God to give an account of their moral conduct upon this Earth. They secretly nurse in their bosom, or openly profess, that they do not really believe there is a place of outer darkness reserved for rebellious, disobedient men who will exist together in hateful contempt for each other, forever banished from the glorious light and love and spirit of God's presence.

The worldly members of the fellowship resent the fact that love is associated with law in the revealed ethics of Jesus Christ. The Corinthian saints were lustfully loose and lawless in their relationship to each other. God called them to the nobler life of love and obedience. In the divinely revealed system of Christian morality, the end of the charge is "love out of a pure heart, a good conscience, and faith unfeigned" (1 Tim. 1:5). This great ethical commission is expressed by John in these words:

> Love not the world, neither the things that are in the world. If
> any man love the world, the love of the Father is not in him.
> For all that is in the world, the lust of the flesh, and the lust of
> the eyes and the vain-glory of life, is not of the Father but is
> of the world. (1 John 2:15–16)

In personal relationships love is the divine command. Worldliness creeps into the church when God's children live by lust rather than by love. The grace of God is forced by their materialistic logic into license for lawless conduct. Paul protested vigorously: "Shall we continue in sin that grace may abound? God forbid" (Rom. 7:1, 2). John pled earnestly with God's children saying, "My little children, these things I write unto you that you may not sin" (1 John 2:1), and he continues his urgent plea:

> Behold what manner of love the Father hath bestowed upon
> us that we should be called the children of God . . . Every one
> that doeth sin doeth also lawlessness. and sin is lawlessness.
> And ye know that he was manifested to take away our sin.
> and in him is no sin. Whosoever abideth in him sinneth not
> . . . Whosoever is begotten of God doeth no sin, because his
> seed abideth in him and he cannot sin, because he is begot-
> ten of God. In this the children of God are manifest, and the
> children of the devil. (1 John 3:1, 4, 6, 9, 10)

There are many modern philosophers, scientists, and theologians, of whom Albert Schweitzer is representative, who interpret the ethics of Jesus in light of His teaching on "last things" (eschatology). They call it an interim (in between, temporary) morality which is too severe and strenuous for prolonged life upon the Earth. They say that Jesus's ethics are based on fear concerning the end of the world and the judgment of the soul after death, rather than on love. They interpret His moral code in eschatological terms, rather than in the terms of abiding love.

What happens when men wrest the Christian morality out of the context of the second coming of Christ, the day of judgment, and the end of the world? What happens when love is so loosely defined that it is not compatible with law and order and obedience? The answer is found in a parable of Jesus:

> But and if that evil servant shall say in his heart, 'My Lord
> delays his coming', and shall begin to smite his fellow ser-
> vants and to eat and drink with the drunken; the lord of that
> servant shall come in a day when he looketh not for him, and
> in an hour that he is not aware of. (Matt. 24:48–50)

Brethren, notice the moral effects of unbelief in the life of the man who loses faith in the promise of the Lord to return. This attitude of worldly immorality is also reflected in the language of Peter:

> In the last days mockers shall come with mockery, walking
> after their own lusts, and saying, Where is the promise of his

> coming? for from the day that our fathers fell asleep all things continue as they were from the beginning of the creation. For this they willfully forget, that there were heavens from of old, and an earth . . . which . . . perished. (2 Pet. 3:3–6)

To all who thus willfully forget, Peter has a warning:

> The day of the Lord will come as a thief; in the which the heavens shall pass away with a great noise, and the elements shall melt with a fervent heat, and the earth and the works that are therein shall be burned up. (2 Pet. 3:10)

Peter pleads for Christian morality on the basis of the doctrine of last things and urges us to live in the strength of the abiding love of God. "Seeing that these things are thus to be dissolved, what manner of persons ought ye to be in all holy living and godliness, looking for and earnestly desiring the coming of the day of God . . . Wherefore, beloved, seeing that ye look for these things, give diligence that ye may be found in peace, without spot and blameless in his sight" (2 Pet. 3:11–12, 14).

In our modern world men are losing sight of moral principles and spiritual values in their feverish competition for economic and political control of the world's affairs. Capitalists and Communists have crucified Christ and Christian virtues in their mad race to the moon. The superior man is the man who gets there first with the most money to stake out his claim. Billions of dollars are being invested in this effort to reach the moon and win worldly prestige. Materialistic, worldly men are boasting that they will soon conquer the limitless expanse of space, which they can never do until they put on immortality, a doctrine which they confidently deny. Traveling at the speed of light, it will take man four and a half years to reach the nearest star. Verily, he will have to become immortal to search to the ends of God's universe. The moon is within easy reach, it seems, but even on the moon man cannot escape from the inevitable reality of facing God in judgment. Only heavenly love will abide in that day when

> . . . the sun shall be darkened and the moon shall not give
> her light, and the stars shall fall from heaven and the powers
> of the heavens shall be shaken; and then shall appear the
> sign of the Son of man in heaven: and then shall all the
> tribes of the earth mourn, and they shall see the Son of man
> coming on the clouds of heaven with power and great glory.
> (Matt. 24:29, 30)

We call to a great city—not Moscow, nor Washington, nor earthly Jerusalem—but the city of God, the New Jerusalem, whose builder and maker is God. This city "hath no need of the sun, neither of the moon to shine upon it: for the glory of God did lighten it, and the lamp thereof is the Lamb" (Rev. 21:23).

What is a nation profited if it gain the moon and lose its soul? And, to all of us who are too proud and worldly to live "soberly, and righteously, and godly in this present world, "we must hasten to say: 'What is a man profited if he gain the whole world, and lose his own soul?'"

Behold the spiritual and moral tragedy of Americans who strive for money so they can pick up the check for admission and cover charge in the carnal atmosphere of gluttonous dining, lascivious dancing, and lustful conversation over cocktail glasses. All of this dining, dancing, and drinking in smoke-filled lounges and dens of homes and the underworld is the ugly outbreaking of the deadly disease of worldliness. It is a disease that cannot be controlled and destroyed by salving the sores with a few sermons on each ugly manifestation that meets the eye. It must be conquered by creating in men a new heart and a spiritual mind.

As long as church members are carnal-minded, we shall continue to see the ugly manifestations of worldliness. We shall not correct the evil of worldliness until we do two things: (1) Call for a new birth, and put a stop to the evil of baptizing carnal-minded, unregenerate people who join churches rather than becoming children of God by the new birth, and (2) discipline with all the power of truth in love those who are members of the Christian fellowship. We live in an undisciplined age. We must train people in the right way. Lawlessness is on every hand. We must, as an act of love, withdraw fellowship and refuse "to keep company, if any man that is named a brother be a fornicator, or covetous, or an idolater, or a reviler, or a drunkard, or an extortioner; with such a one no not to eat" (1 Cor. 5:11).

But, in harmony with the moral law: "Let all that you do be done in love" (1 Cor. 16:14). And, if withdrawal of fellowship is necessary to save a soul from death, let us have the courage to do it. But God forbid that we do so hatefully. Paul says: "Note that man, that ye have no company with him, to the end that he may be ashamed. And yet count him not as an enemy, but admonish him as a brother" (2 Thess. 3:14, 15).

In conclusion, we direct your thoughts to Paul's words to Titus:

> The grace of God hath appeared, bringing salvation to all men, instructing us, to the intent that, denying ungodliness and worldly lusts, we should live soberly and righteously and godly in this present world; looking for the blessed hope and appearing of the glory of the great God and our Savior Jesus Christ; who gave himself for us, that he might redeem us from all iniquity, and purify unto himself a people for his own possession, zealous of good works. (Titus 2:11–14)

"Having therefore these promises, beloved, let us cleanse ourselves from all defilements of flesh and spirit, perfecting holiness in the fear of God" (2 Cor. 7:1).

"Statement of Acknowledgement of Racial Prejudice and Proposals for Improving Race Relations in Churches of Christ"

We the undersigned individual Christians acknowledge the sin of racial prejudice which has existed in Churches of Christ and church-related institutions and businesses. Because we love the church of Jesus Christ and want to see her fully committed to the principles of Spiritual Equality and racial justice for all persons, we plead for the end of discrimination in all of its forms in the life of the church. To this goal the following proposals are directed:

I. Re: Local Church Activities

1. Plan race relations workshop: for church leaders (preachers, elders, deacons, teachers) in every region of the United States.

2. Encourage Christians to attend interracial meetings and worship with churches attended by Christians of other races.
3. Begin serious educational programs in local churches including sermons, to inform the brethren of the Bible teaching on racial discrimination.
4. Integrate local congregations as these opportunities exist, seeking to achieve the meaningful involvement of Christians of all races in the total program of the church.
5. Publicize the fact that the church is open to persons of all races, if this is true.
6. Plan all cooperative efforts in evangelism and benevolence to include Christians of all races.
7. Evaluate all missions programs to ascertain they are based on genuine fraternity, and not paternalism.

II. Re: Church-Related Institutions

1. Increase efforts at Christian colleges to recruit more nonwhite students (by offering more scholarships for them).
2. Consider hiring qualified black teachers and other non-academic personnel at Christian colleges.
3. Consider appointment of blacks for boards of trustees
4. Totally integrate all social activities at Christian colleges.
5. Study the possibility of introducing courses of learning on black culture and Afro-American history.
6. Sponsor a race relations workshop on every Christian college campus (making available printed materials on this issue to all students).
7. Urge Christian College lectureship directors and committees to plan entire lectureships on the theme of spiritual equality ("Oneness in Christ" or a similar theme).
8. Integrate children's homes, homes for aged, and Christian camps and seek to have integrated staffs, boards of trustees, and counselors at camp.

9. Open all Bible Chairs to Christians of all races and seek to integrate staff and all social activities.
10. Integrate the staff of Campus Evangelism. Program and develop interracial materials.

III. Re: HERALD OF TRUTH (Only national mass-media effort of Churches of Christ)

1. Speak courageously on the sin of racial discrimination on both radio and TV Programs.
2. Use blacks in TV film series in various roles (not simply subservient roles).
3. Use black speakers on radio and TV speakers in the course of a year.

IV. Re: Publishing Companies and Christian Bookstores

1. Solicit articles from qualified black writers and ask them to prepare articles on various subjects.
2. Publish more articles on the issue of racial discrimination and injustice.
3. Publish more articles on news of activities of black churches and Christians and run photographs of these activities when available.
4. Develop Bible school literature, books, filmstrips and slides to include proper representation of all races—to aid in the process of identification for minority groups.
5. Urge Christian publishers and Christian bookstores to seek out qualified persons of all races to assume front-office jobs as well as the other jobs usually assigned to minority groups.

V. Re: Christian-Owned Businesses

1. Urge employment of qualified persons of all races.

2. Plan in-training programs to qualify members of minority groups for jobs other than dead-end jobs, offering them the opportunity—if they are qualified—for positions of supervision and management.

VI. Re: All Christians

1. Affirm without equivocation that equal opportunities in housing, jobs, and schooling should be granted to all persons in our democratic society.
2. Employ one's influence—political, social, economic, and religious—to support these convictions on equal rights and opportunities.

June 26, 1968
Atlanta, Georgia

Signed by: Jimmy Allen, Jim Bevis, Walter E. Burch, Robert L. Butler, John Allen Chalk, Ray F. Chester, Dennis Crowder, Jennings Davis Jr., Booker T. Ellis, Dwain Evans, Franklin D. Florence, Humphrey Foutz, Robert M. Fulmer, George Gurganus, Andrew J. Hairston, Maurice Haynes, R. N. Hogan, G. P. Holt, Richard Horton, David Jones Jr., Eugene Lawton, William C. Martin, Prentice A. Meador Jr., Woodie Morrison, James W. Nichols, Robert W. Randolph, Wesley Reagan, James Robert Ross, Landon B. Saunders, Carl Spain, Lawrence (Bud) Stumbaugh, James W. Thompson, Orum Lee Trone Sr., R. C. Wells, Cled Wimbish

"Address by Lawrence L. (Bud) Stumbaugh"

Tonight I am going to inflict some red-hot realism upon you. I intend to raise a howl of calamity about the past, present, and persistent failure of the church to be what it ought to be. I cannot approach the foul and violent crimes of so-called "Christianity" in hushed tones. I cannot smooth over the church's ugly history of hypocrisy by preaching pleasant and pious platitudes. Bearing upon my conscience at this moment is the realization that one does not have to be grossly wicked to be immoral—just spineless. That is why my attitude is one of explosive urgency. That is why my concern is with what I *must* say, not with what people may think.

Some may say, "You are an angry young man." To that charge I reply, Paul commands that we be angry, without sinning, and I believe it is far past time for righteous indignation. Some may say, "You are a demagogue, an extremist, a fanatic, a heretic." To that accusation I answer:

That is what Galileo was called as he stood before his inquisitors saying, "The earth does move!" That's what was said about Martin Luther when he nailed his 95 theses on the door of the powerful Roman church. Some may say, "You are rebellious; you are a trouble-maker." To such I point out that Jesus's accusers said, as recorded at Luke 23:5, "He stirs up the people . . ." I also remember Paul and Silas were accused of turning the world upside down (Acts 17:6).

Now I am not placing myself, in mentality or morals, on a par with Galileo, Luther, Jesus, Paul, or Silas. But I do believe that as they were right, I am right. My position is not one of race against race, black against white. It is one of right against wrong. I cannot be silent. I cannot be calm. I will not excuse. I will not compromise. I will not be affable and easy-going. I will not be intimidated. With such oceans of icebergs around me, I *must* be hot. I must present the unadulterated and sometimes scandalizing truth!

And the truth about this matter of race relations is that, contrary to what the majority of Caucasians have been thinking and saying, the major domestic difficulty in America cannot be properly labeled the "Negro problem." Basically, the problem is, and always has been, a *white* problem.

Yes, white religionists began and are responsible for perpetuating America's racial crisis. You see, it was mainly white churchmen who more than three hundred years ago forcefully brought black people from the continent of Africa to this land. These captives were stacked together in holds of ships with no more regard than one would have in stacking lumber in piles. The ships were floating death traps where more than sixty million unwilling passengers ate, slept, urinated, defecated, vomited, and died in the cramped and disease-infected quarters.

By comparison, the Nazi genocide of this century seems almost like a game of hide-and-seek. Why those of us who are the descendants of the slave runners and slave owners of yesteryear should be shocked at Hitler's theory of the master race, and his consequent debasement and cruel treatment of those he termed inferior, is one of the inconsistencies of our reasoning processes I will never understand.

But our forefathers excused their behavior on the grounds that these "poor," "ignorant," "pagan savages" were fortunate, under whatever conditions, to be brought to a country which would "bless" them with such "civilized" and "Christian" environment and association. It is strange, indeed, how ungrateful many of these blacks were, for they staged mutinies, leaped into the sea to drown while still chained together, and tried every known method of suicide to keep from accepting the "blessing" of living in this "Christian" nation.

And no wonder they chose death, for who among us would prefer to live as the slaves were forced to live? Working but never enjoying the fruits of his labor. Adults cruelly beaten with whips. Little children denied culture and education while being forced to work in the fields. Pretty black women raped by pitiless white men. Mothers sobbing as their strong children were taken from them and sold to the highest bidder, thus breaking up the family. Parents actually praying God would cause the little child developing in the mother's womb to be born deformed so it would have no value on the labor market and would not be forcefully separated from its family by being sold to whoever offered the most money.

By making laws in direct contradiction to the great themes and pronouncements of the Bible, white Christians broke almost every rule in the one book they claimed to follow. In determining each state's population the U. S. Congress decreed that black people be counted as only three-fifths of a person. How could anyone dare take away two-fifths of the humanity of someone created in the image of God! The very ones who taught others the Bible's emphasis on the sanctity of the family made it illegal for slaves to marry and forced them to vent their natural physical desires as an animal of the field would. And the Supreme Court of the United States, in its Dred Scott decision, affirmed that the Negro had no rights that the white man was bound to respect. It is downright unbelievable that anyone who claimed to live by the Golden Rule could hand down or follow a pronouncement declaring another human being had no rights to be respected. But our so-called Christian nation, dominated by white supremacists, did.

Then came supposed liberation from slavery through the Emancipation Act of 1863. But as Henrietta Buckmaster put it, "With Appomatox [*sic*], four million black people in the South owned their skins and nothing more." Slaves had been denied education. They had had no money to save. They owned no property. They were not just ill-prepared, but non-prepared to face their "new" life. Since these slaves did not, upon being freed, immediately possess the knowledge and skill of others in society, the lie of innate inferiority was again spread by the "good, white Christians" to justify placing human being in bondage. Whites had denied blacks all the essentials for getting ahead in life and then denounced the black race for not possessing these essentials as if it were the black race's fault. The black man was blinded by the white man so to speak, and then condemned for not being able to see. The very people who had amputated his legs were now criticizing the black man for being a cripple.

Out of this situation was born the philosophy that the races should be segregated. Since black people were uneducated and uncultured, they were supposedly unfit and unable to receive the benefits of education and culture such as whites had access to. To mix the races in the quest for these things would supposedly pull the so-called superior whites down to the low level of blacks; thus, blacks continued to find themselves denied the tools which were producing a more affluent white society. The tragic *results* of deprivation and segregation were used as an argument for the continuation of deprivation and segregation. This same twisted and immoral logic is still used today in defense of the continuation of segregation.

As already suggested, so-called white Christianity was and is the main cause of the racial problems we face today. The church started the doctrine of race separation and worked so vigorously for it that segregation became a part of Christian dogma. White supremacy was literally defended with Bible in hand. Passages of Scripture were so twisted out of context until even today, to many people, the true defender of "pure religion" is he who screams most vociferously for eternal separation of the races in the church and general society. But while claiming to uphold the teachings of the Bible, the segregationist's stance has been in direct conflict with what the Bible really teaches.

For example: Philippians 2:3 says " . . . in humility count others *better* than yourselves." But many white churchmen teach that Negroes are inferior and never will be as good as whites, thus violating not only the scriptures, but also showing their ignorance of anthropology, psychology, sociology, biology, and ethnology which have never proved any race to be naturally or innately inferior or superior to another.

Philippians 2:4 teaches that each of us should ". . . look not only to his own interests, but also to the interest of others"—but most whites excuse themselves for, say, not serving Negroes in their places of business by claiming it would lose them customers, thus showing they are more interested in their own well-being and profits than in looking out for the other fellow. Whites often say they are opposed to integration because of the effect it might have on their children, but usually fail to show the same concern over the effect of segregation on little black children.

James 2:1 teaches us to "show no partiality as you hold the faith of our Lord Jesus Christ . . ." But I can name several congregations who are so partial to, and so respectful of, white skin that their black brothers and sisters who share similar doctrinal beliefs are either turned away completely from the assemblies or forced to sit on the back row or in the balcony.

These same congregations, when mailing announcements of a Vacation Bible School or some other program designed to influence the community, will systematically skip streets on which Negroes reside. This is done deliberately. In door-knocking campaigns to stimulate interest in evangelistic meetings, these same streets are knowingly excluded.

And many, even of those few Southern congregations who have a minute percentage of black people worshipping with them, are not completely sold on the ideas of non-partiality. For when it is evident that the neighborhood where the church's building is located is becoming a predominantly Negro neighborhood, usually the whites run as fast as they can to the outskirts of town, buy up several acres of land, put up a new building, sell the old building to the "colored brethren" or to some other religious body so the newly acquired debts can be paid. Such churches sit back and pat themselves on the back for the fine progress they have made. I do not call a move motivated by such factors "progress"; I call it moral bankruptcy! And when this splitting of fellowship is advertised on a double-page spread (as recently happened in Nashville), enabling all to see this horrible degeneracy, it makes me want to throw up.

But perhaps the most flagrantly violated passage has been Matthew 7:12, the Golden Rule. Since I do not want to be called "boy" when I am sixty-five years old, since I do not want to be called "nigger," "darkie," "nigra," or any other disparaging name, it is wrong for me to call black people by such names.

Since I would not want to be turned away from church assemblies because of the color of my skin, I cannot turn others away for that reason.

Since I would not like to be turned away from church-related colleges because of the color of my skin, I cannot treat others that way.

Since I would not want to tell my little girl she will have to hold back her biological urge because there are no bathrooms for her race, since I would not want to tell my little girl that she is not allowed to sit up front near the bus driver, since I would not want my little girl's heart broken when I have to explain that she is not welcome to use the so-called "public" park or swimming pool, since I would not want my little girl to sleep in a cold cramped car on a trip because there are no motels that will accept her, since I would not want my little girl to grow up without the respected title of Miss or Mrs., since I would not want my little girl to grow up with the nagging thought that "most people do not like me," I cannot—by my failure to speak out and work against— aid and abet a system which thrusts just such conditions on other precious little girls.

Now I am well aware that many of these forms of injustice no longer openly exist. But I am concerned over the fact that this disgusting discrimination still lingers in some places. Even more, I am concerned that what few improvements have been made in race relations have not come about because white Churches of Christ repented and brought forth righteous works suitable for a group which is aware of its ugly past and wants to change it. Scoffers have abundant reasons to cast aspersions at us for our colossal shortcomings. We have been found deficient in love on the one hand and courage on the other.

W. E. B. DuBois, American educator and writer who was of Negro descent, was a prophet of doom who proved correct in his castigation of Caucasian churchmen. He denied that this group would ever take any arduous action to alleviate misery, wrongdoing, and suffering among black people by saying: "Of all the groups devoted to social uplift, I have least hope in the white Christian ministers." It, of course, goes without saying that if the ministers who encourage and influence the different churches do not take a stand for helping the downtrodden, precious few of the members will either.

Perhaps Negro entertainer Dick Gregory best sums up the church's failure to be a vitalizing force in shaping human morals in the area of race relations. Mr. Gregory shocked 3,500 teenage Lutherans gathered for a convention in Washington, DC, by the following reply to their question, did he think the church was still a power that could do something to benefit the Negro: "My personal conviction is I believe it's too late. We had the Civil War. Then one hundred years later it would have been a great thing had the church stepped forward with leadership to free a great many of the oppressed people in America. This would have been a feather in God's cap. We would have said, 'Thank God.' The church has failed in such a horrible way that now everyone seems to say, 'Thank the Supreme Court.'"

Black people do not find it possible to thank the Church of Christ for the better treatment they have been accorded. Thank the schools, the government, the labor organizations, the civil rights groups, some employers, the Supreme Court—but not the church.

Of course, the rationalization for the church's failure to speak out and act is that segregation/integration is a political issue and the church cannot therefore involve itself. Such dribble [*sic*]! Such inconsistency!

In 1960, in papers and magazines owned and edited by members of the church, much was published in condemnation of the candidacy of John F. Kennedy for United States President. Pulpit preachments, bulletin articles, special announcements, radio and television programs, bulk mail-outs on church letterheads, and other means were used to denounce Kennedy's political aspirations because of his religion. Writers and speakers defended the church's involvement in a political contest with the explanation that spiritual issues were at stake. They admitted it was a political matter, but they said its religious ramifications made church involvement imperative.

But now, just because both political parties are enmeshed in the controversial issue of race relations, it has become wrong to be involved. Editors, preachers, and churches have grown strangely silent. No pronouncements, few articles, less sermons. If historians a thousand years from now were unable to read any documents other than pamphlets, papers, and magazines written by members of the Church of Christ, they would not be able to discern that America even had a racial problem in the middle years of the twentieth century. They would learn that the church had worked diligently to keep a Catholic from becoming president, but they would find almost no indication that the church had worked hard to assure that black people were treated right. Yet the Bible nowhere calls on disciples to work for freedom of religion. In fact, early Christianity thrived without this freedom so many were working to protect during the Nixon–Kennedy campaign. But the Bible throughout does call for love, peace, fellowship, and justice among all men. Somehow the Church of Christ says more on a presidential race than on race relations!

And only last fall the Church of Christ got involved in another political contest—right here in Nashville. I refer to the liquor-by-the-drink referendum. Justification for involvement was that a moral or spiritual issue was again at stake. Now I do not take lightly anyone's concern over the dangers of intoxicants; many of these dangers are real. However, I do believe it is the height of inconsistency to preach about the dangers of liquor during the fervor of political activity over the subject and not preach about the evil of racial injustice when the subject of race relations is likewise uppermost in the minds of almost everyone.

Why did we not give out tracts on street corners in 1954 supporting not just the need for compliance with law, but also pointing out that the higher law of love made it imperative that we do the right for which the US Supreme Court justices were calling? Why did we not, back then, or decades sooner, send our teenagers to all the shopping centers with thousands of handbills to stick under automobile windshield wipers? Why didn't concerned Christians form private groups to work for integration?

Was it because race relations was a political question which the church could not speak or act on without committing sin? No! Churches of Christ felt they could give out tracts and handbills, preach sermons, and write articles during a presidential vote and during a liquor vote. And if they had been consistent they could have done the same thing concerning race relations, with much more biblical justification. When extremely influential preachers and writers begin to stand as vigorously for a change in the racial picture as they have in some of these safe areas which do not bring the wrath of their congregations upon them, then we will begin to see some concrete improvements in a very immoral situation.

This matter of working for the defeat of a legal proposal calling for the sale of liquor by the drink brings up another inconsistent stance many have taken. Almost every time a new bill is presented before the state or national legislature, the cry is raised that "you can't legislate morals." Isn't that what those opposed to the liquor-by-the-drink bill were trying to do? If morals cannot be legislated, then why do we bother having laws against speeding, bank robbery, or murder?

Of course, it's true morals cannot be legislated. But behavior can be regulated, and that is what society is trying to do when it passes laws against speeding, bank robbery, murder, and racial discrimination. True, laws cannot make you love me, but they can make you serve me food when I am hungry and have the money to pay for it. Laws can make you quit lynching me, and after all, when you have a rope around my neck, I do not really care if you remove that rope because of love or law, favor or fear, just so long as you remove that rope. I favor more and better legislation in the area of human rights, because I know it can make us treat one another better. I also know better behavior can be learned, and if the law forces me to practice goodness long enough, I might just learn to do good naturally and even like it. I did not like spinach as a child, but I had to eat it because my folks laid down that law to me. You know, I finally learned to like it!

Concerning another inconsistency regarding law, let me say it is high time for white Christians to decide if law breaking is good or bad, right or wrong. Too many whites applaud George Wallace for standing in the schoolhouse door to keep out black students the law said to enter, but then get upset when Martin Luther King defies a court injunction. And if we can justify law breaking and destruction of property by labeling as heroes our forefathers who staged the "Boston Tea Party," should not we also label as heroes those who today destroy property in hopes of forcing a settlement of their grievances? If the midnight ride of Paul Revere and his shouting of "To arms, to arms, the British are coming" was a glorious and patriotic call for freedom, then don't condemn blacks for calling for arms in order to fight for their freedom. If our forefathers did not have to wait for the courts and ruling powers of their day to alleviate misery and injustice, then blacks have as much right today to start a revolution in order to achieve justice, without waiting for the powers that be to grant it.

Of course, the church is pretty inconsistent in calling for nonviolence in the first place. People laugh at the lie we tell when we claim to be a peace-loving people. This country of churches is the only nation I know who has, on the basis of official national policy, tried to wipe out its indigenous population. And somehow whenever the "pagan enemy" was violent (usually for self-protection), it was always worse than when the "Christian" US forces were violent. For example, whenever the US Cavalry won a battle, it was called a victory. But whenever the Indians won it was called a massacre. Why the difference?

Haven't we always tried to justify our "white" violence? Our military leaders justified dropping a bomb on yellow and brown people of Hiroshima, completely burning 55,000 of the 75,000 existing homes and killing 78,150 innocent citizens because it was done "to save American lives." Similar fate came to civilians in Nagasaki. You see, the policy of this nation, and basically that of the church, has always been that violence is right if a noble and just and higher purpose is served. Now black people are beginning to echo this same philosophy; they believe the lives of their children's children are more important than a few dilapidated tenements, so some of them feel justified in saying "Burn, baby, burn." If violence is so wrong, why do I keep hearing statements from many pulpits defending "our patriotic boys who are in Vietnam fighting for freedom?" If God allows us to be violent, even to the point of taking lives, as long as the cause is just, then violent blacks who fight for racial freedom should have the blessings and prayers of the church as do our boys overseas. But if God meant what he said about loving the enemy, turning the other cheek, and returning good for evil, then let this be preached with equal fervor to the white military machine as it is to the black power organization.

What is the biblical position in regard to violence? Well, let me state unequivocally, I believe the Bible teaches pacifism. I am a pacifist through and through. I believe in, teach and practice nonviolence. I will not kill, for I believe to do so would violate the biblical doctrine of love, both of friend and foe. However, this does not mean I am timid, a pushover, weak, reticent, or inactive. Yes, I believe in love, but I also believe true love is accompanied by beneficent power, or it is nothing more than anemic sentiment.

Jesus loved everybody and never killed anyone, but he was certainly not a passive person. He leveled a scathing denunciation against the Pharisees, and he drove the money-changers out of the temple with a whip. I believe that today we need the same kind of love Jesus possessed. Sometimes it takes rebuking, pressure, and force to make people do right, both for their own good and the good of others. That is why I sometimes spank my little girl, and according to Hebrews chapter 12, the reason God sometimes spanks or chastises us in order to make us do right.

It is a sad but historically true fact that domineering, privileged powers that oppress do not willingly give up their position of dominance. Evil individuals and governments have always had to be pressured into doing right. It took pressure to make Pharoah of the Old Testament do right. It took pressure to make the King of England give the American colonists representation for their taxation, and I have previously mentioned the praise we heap on our forefathers who exerted this pressure. Read the history of the struggle for woman suffrage in America. Note especially the tumultuous years 1913–19 and see how American mothers and grandmothers picketed the White House, demonstrated with placards filled with messages to President Wilson, pitched tents with the threat of camping out on the White House lawn until Congress gave women the right to vote, and finally, see how many of these mothers and grandmothers were thrown into jail for their activities. But it won them suffrage! And today, women like Susan B. Anthony, Julia Ward Howe, Lucy Stone, Carrie Chapman Catt, and Anna Howard Shaw are heroes. Well, I tell you proudly and with no reservations that men like Martin Luther King, Medgar Evers, Whitney Young, Jr., James Farmer, and scores of others are heroes in my eyes today. This does not mean I agree with everything they have said or done, but it does mean I appreciate the way they have worked so actively and, in the main non-violently, in their unceasing efforts to secure freedom for the oppressed and to make the oppressor do right.

And although many whites and some blacks are sure to say that demonstrations, boycotts, and other pressure tactics only create animosity and set race relations back, I think the facts prove otherwise. The 1960 sit-ins desegregated lunch counters in more than 150 cities within twelve months. While I was still a student in high school in Selma, Alabama, the 1956 bus boycott in Montgomery ended segregation on the buses of not only that city, but in almost every city of the South. Without the events in Birmingham in 1963 there would probably have been no passage of the Civil Rights Act of 1964. The 1965 Selma movement brought about the enactment of the voting rights law which has helped to register over a million black voters since its passage. In 1967, marches and protests in Louisville, Kentucky, brought about the passage of an open-housing [law] in that city. On and on the list of improvements go, and probably not a single one of them would have been achieved without pressure.

"But," someone says, "if people are doing right only because of pressure, of what value is that motive to them?" My answer is to again remind you that I learned to like spinach because I was made to eat it. Many people will find that integration and fairness are not so bad after all, if only they can be made to practice such. Many things my daughter does now because I spank her if she does not, she will later do because she sees it is right and even enjoyable.

Of course, just as pressure that parents exert in disciplining their offspring will sometimes cause hurt feelings, temper tantrums, and emotional outbursts from these children, hurt feelings and flare-ups will often occur when civil rights pressure is exerted. But as parents are not to blame for their children's temper tantrums which occur when proper pressure has been applied out of love and concern for both the children's and the rest of the family's welfare, neither are civil rights activists who exert pressure in proper ways and for proper motives at fault for bringing to fore the pent-up prejudice, violence, and hate of racial bigots. To blame those who pressure the white bigots for justice, for the hateful reactions of those bigots, is like blaming a doctor for a cancer found upon making exploratory surgery upon his patient. The doctor did not cause the cancer. He merely uncovered what was already in existence. I believe many peaceful civil rights groups have been accused of fostering hate and violence, when in reality they have merely uncovered the latent and explosive bigotry that was already deep down in the hearts of rabid white people.

And although those who demonstrate, boycott, and use other forms of "spankings" out of concern and love will be branded as un-Christian and violent hatemongers, such pressure is certainly not sinful; and indeed, to sit back and passively accept evil without using every logical and legitimate means to eradicate it is to lend aid and comfort to wrong; such passiveness itself becomes sin (James 4:17).

Thus I believe that at every opportunity, Christians of color ought to use all proper pressure and every moral means of force to assure that white Christians begin to practice the love and justice they have been preaching for so long. To use a phrase others have used, I am in favor of "black power," for it seems this is what it will take to make a degenerate society do right. Do not be shocked that I call for "black power," for power, properly understood, is merely having the strength and ability to accomplish aims. It is the force and energy necessary to bring about change, whether that change be political, social, or moral. From this standpoint, black power is not only good, but imperative, if the bigotry and prejudice of this nation and the church is to be eliminated. Again, I remind you, it is a historical fact that a privileged majority never willingly gives in to an oppressed minority.

I am afraid that if black people do not, out of love and concern, employ the right kind of "love" power to make the church do right, then we will continue upon our present course of prejudice and bigotry. Black power is not just black people's hope for justice and equality. It is white people's hope for personal morality and salvation.

I end with the plea that black people use black power more humanely and morally than have white people in whose hands white power has resided for so long.

SUGGESTED GUIDELINES FOR IMPROVING RACE RELATIONS

1. Call an interracial meeting of church leaders to discuss and implement remedial actions as soon as possible against obvious practices of racial discrimination.
2. Preachers should immediately begin to preach some biblical sermons on the subject—not sermons to justify our sinful positions but sermons telling the truth of the matter.
3. Conduct interracial work projects such as personal work teams workshops, community service projects, etc., so Christians can come to know each other as persons and not simply as "members" of a racial group.
4. Prepare congregations for integration. Since segregation was planned we must plan to get rid of it. Too often elders and ministers will welcome Negroes to a white congregation if they come, but they do nothing to prepare the church for this. A serious educational program on the truth of the gospel on race relations should be launched immediately in every congregation.
5. Have more race relations workshops at other congregations, especially white churches. We realize that this is but a small start, and we must all continually work at the problem.
6. Correct existing segregated church-related establishments, such as the "Hobby Shop," camps, church-related businesses such as publishing houses and bookstores. It is not a sin to hire a Negro clerk in church-related bookstores.
7. Hold smaller interracial group fellowships on a regular basis (monthly).
8. Plan teaching ads on the race problem on radio, TV and newspapers.
9. Encourage Christian school officials to have a lectureship with race relations as a theme and invite a cross-section of Negro and white speakers.

10. Provide a speaker's bureau, making available a group of men to conduct race relations workshops in churches.

11. Plan to worship at a church of another race, either as a visitor or permanently.

12. Clearly indicate that the church is open for men of all races. Many leaders will not agree to this, but it is quite embarrassing for a Christian to go to a church where he is not wanted. Negro Christians do not wish to force themselves upon anyone—so a clearly marked "White Only" sign would be sufficient. Another way would be for congregations in an area to publish a full-page ad in the newspaper to affirm their position.

13. Negroes should develop plans to be independent—building their own buildings, buying their own songbooks, refusing to buy church buildings vacated by the "white brethren."

14. Compile a suggested booklist on the subject of race relations.

15. Show disapproval by withdrawing fellowship from those congregations and/or individuals who refuse the Christian way in this matter, in keeping with New Testament principles.

SHATTERING THE ILLUSION

How African American Churches of Christ Moved from Segregation to Independence

ISBN 978-0-89112-228-9   240 pages

Wes Crawford

The story of how a pivotal 1968 event shattered the illusion of racial unity in Churches of Christ.

From the late 19th century to the dawn of the civil rights movement, Black and White members of Churches of Christ perpetuated an illusion of racial unity by playing their long-established roles in Southern society. For decades this illusion was protected through denominational journals, lectureships, and schools. Just as the civil rights movement was forcing Americans to deal with generations of racism, the events surrounding the closing of the Nashville Christian Institute revealed a secret that had long remained hidden: two racially defined factions with their own customs, identities, and views on race relations existed within Churches of Christ.

The public spectacle that ensued shattered the illusion of unity. And since the 1968 civil rights case entered the courts, the distance between these two racial factions has grown. This important book tells this story with compelling grace and insight, concluding that if these two racial factions are ever to realize meaningful unity, they must find common ground, not only in questions of race but also in issues of theology.

"Through extensive research and unflinching analysis, Wes Crawford recounts the story of the creation of Black and White Churches of Christ in America. *Shattering the Illusion* will certainly shatter illusions about race in Churches of Christ and could help open a way forward for reconciliation and closer relations."
—**Douglas A. Foster,** author of *Renewing Christian Unity*

1-877-816-4455 toll free
www.acupressbooks.com

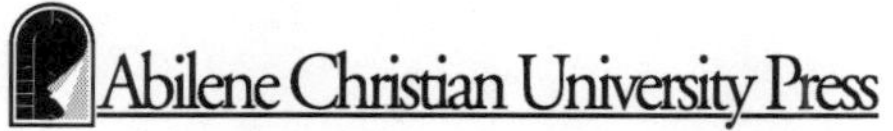

FAITHFUL DEFIANCE

Marshall Keeble's Life and Legacy

ISBN 978-1-68426-214-4   160 pages

C. Leonard Allen, editor

Marshall Keeble, the premier evangelist in twentieth-century Churches of Christ, used his remarkable gifts, toughness, and tactical navigation of the Black-White divide to baptize as many as 40,000.

His message was simple, but his life was more complicated than many have thought. His commitment to evangelism was unwavering, and he wanted nothing to get in the way of it. He championed racial self-help and considered politics of little value. He raised up hundreds of congregations and mentored powerful sons and grandsons in the faith, including Fred Gray, the famous civil rights attorney.

Faithful Defiance recounts the remarkable story of Keeble's life, revealing fresh insights into how his life and legacy continue to challenge the present day.

"We best understand our times and ourselves by looking to history and to giants of the faith. This volume is a shining example of high-impact historical analysis and biography informing our current divisive times."

—Michael O. Emerson, Chavanne Fellow in Religion and Public Policy, Baker Institute for Public Policy, Rice University, and coauthor of *The Religion of Whiteness*

"What an encompassing and engulfing look into the legacy of an historical figure whose influence continues to shape our brotherhood today! Walking through Marshall Keeble's life using various contextual lenses is insightful, inspirational, and impactful."

—Jonathan Morrison, minister, Cedar Crest Church of Christ, Dallas, Texas

DIVERSITY MATTERS

Race, Ethnicity, and the Future of Christian Higher Education

ISBN 978-0-89112-454-2   336 pages

Karen A. Longman, editor

Today, no institution can ignore the need for deep conversations about race and ethnicity. But colleges and universities face a unique set of challenges as they explore these topics. *Diversity Matters* offers leaders a roadmap as they think through how their campuses can serve all students well. Each chapter includes important discussion questions for administration, faculty, and staff.

"*Diversity Matters* is a welcome offering not just in the realm of evangelical Christian higher education, but also in the realm of evangelical Christianity as a whole. Through it, the contributors clearly and courageously address the why, what, and how of developing institutions where racial and ethnic diversity can flourish in ways that benefit the institutions and honor God."

—Bishop Claude Alexander, pastor of The Park Church, Charlotte, NC

"We are at a critical moment in Christian education in regard to diversity. With the demographics of our nation changing dramatically every year, it is imperative that the church and Christian institutions of higher learning keep pace with this changing reality. To that end, *Diversity Matters* offers sound advice to all who wish to join in this necessary progress."

—Noel Castellanos, President, Camino Alliance

1-877-816-4455 toll free
www.acupressbooks.com

Abilene Christian University Press